THE GREATEST HONKY-TONKS IN TEXAS

OTHER BOOKS BY BILL PORTERFIELD

Texas Rhapsody
A Loose Herd of Texans
The Book of Dallas (with Evelyn Oppenheimer)
LBJ Country

THE GREATEST HONKY-TONKS IN TEXAS

BILL PORTERFIELD

TAYLOR PUBLISHING COMPANY
Dallas, Texas

Interior Art and Maps: Harvey Shirai

Dance Steps: John Reed, Dance Instructor, Longhorn Ballroom, Dallas

A special thanks to the following for the Honky-Tonk photographs:
Evans Caglage, Jay Godwin, Tim Bullard, Henry Bargas, Carlos Rosales, W. G. Roberts.

Local Option Map compiled by Wholesale Beer Distributors of Texas.

The sketches of Aunt Earline, Bois D'Arc Sam, The Midnight Dancer, and J. A. and Lupe are taken from *Texas Rhapsody*, copyright © 1975, 1976, 1978, 1979, 1980, 1981 by Bill Porterfield. Reprinted by permission of Holt, Rinehart and Winston, publishers.

Copyright © 1983 by Taylor Publishing Company
1550 W. Mockingbird Lane, Dallas, Texas 75235

All rights reserved. Except for short quotes excerpted by reviewers, no part of this publication may be reproduced in any form or by any means, written or electronic, without permission in writing from the publisher.

Library of Congress Catalog Card Number: 83-18011

Printed in the United States of America

ACKNOWLEDGMENTS

Now and then in my columns in the *Dallas Times Herald* I have touched upon some of the folk who dance through this book. I thank the paper for allowing me to expand upon them in another medium. While I'm at it, I guess I ought to take my hat off to the honky-tonk people themselves, since it's their stories I've lifted.

Every effort has been made to locate, identify and credit the authors, composers, and publishers quoted. Acknowledgments are indicated below. In cases where the current proprietor of copyright is unknown or has not been ascertainable by inquiries or research, acknowledgment has been made to the source from which the material is quoted. Any inadvertent omissions or errors will be corrected in future editions.

I wish to thank the authors and publishers of the following literary works from which passages have been quoted:
"The Glamour of the Gay Night Life: The Classic Honky-Tonk" by James Ward Lee, Texas Folklore Society Publication, 1982; *Country Music, U.S.A.* by Bill C. Malone, American Folklore Society, University of Texas Press, 1968; "The Passions of the Common Man" by Larry L. King, *Texas Monthly*, August 1976; "Bury My Heart at Wounded Neck" by James Ward Lee, Texas Folklore Society Publication, XL, 1976; *Lone Star: A History of Texas and the Texans* by T. R. Fehrenbach, published by American Legacy Press by arrangement with Macmillan Publishing Co., Inc.; *The Great Plains States of America* by Neal R. Peirce, Copyright 1973, 1972 by Neal R. Peirce, All Rights Reserved, W. W. Norton Company, Inc.; *Saturday Night at Gilleys* by Bob Claypool, Copyright 1980 by Bob Claypool, Delilah/Grove Press, Inc. Larry McMurtry's quote is from *Panhandle Cowboy* by John R. Erickson, by permission of the University of Nebraska Press, Copyright 1981, University of Nebraska Press. Sidney Lanier's quote is from William Corner's "San Antonio de Bexar, 1890" (reprinted by Mary Ann Noonan-Guerra, 1980).

Thanks also to the writers and publishers of the following songs from which lyrics have been quoted:
"Waltz Across Texas" by Talmadge Tubb, Copyright 1965 by Ernest Tubb Music, Inc. (BMI), International Copyright Secured, Made in U.S.A., All Rights Reserved; "Honky Tonk Blues" by Hank Williams, Copyright 1948 by Fred Rose Music, Inc., Copyright renewed 1975, assigned to Fred Rose Music, Inc., and Hiriam Music for the U.S.A. only, all rights outside the U.S.A. controlled by Fred Rose Music, Inc., International Copyright Secured, Made. in U.S.A., All Rights Reserved; "Still Doin' Time" by Michael P. Heeney and John E. Moffat, Copyright 1981 by Cedarwood Publishing Co., Inc., International Copyright Secured, Made in U.S.A., All Rights

Reserved; "A Country Boy Can Survive" by Hank Williams, Jr., recorded on "Pressure Is On," 1981 Electra/Asylum (Warner); "M-O-T-H-E-R" by Howard Johnson and Theodore Morse, Copyright 1915 (Renewed 1943) by Leo Feist, Inc., International Copyright Secured, Made in U.S.A., All Rights Reserved; "Mother Was a Lady" by Edward B. Marks and Joseph W. Stern, Copyright 1896 by Joseph W. Stern and Co.; "Could I Have This Dance?" by Wayland Holyfield and Bob House, Copyright 1980 by Bibo Music Publishers (c/o The Welk Music Group, Santa Monica, Calif. 90401) and Onhisown Music (c/o OAS Music Group, Inc., 805 18th Avenue South, Nashville, Tenn. 37203), International Copyright Secured, Made in U.S.A., All Rights Reserved; "Wild Side of Life" by W. Warren and A. A. Carter, Copyright 1952 (Renewed 1980) by Unart Music Corporation, International Copyright Secured, Made in U.S.A., All Rights Reserved; "Redneck Girl" by the Bellamy Brothers, Copyright 1982 by Famous Music Corporation and Bellamy Brothers Music, International Copyright Secured, Made in U.S.A., All Rights Reserved.

Also, "It Wasn't God Who Made Honky-Tonk Angels" by J. D. Miller, Copyright 1952 by Peer International Corporation, Copyright Renewed, Used by Permission, All Rights Reserved; "Cigareetes, Whuskey and Wild, Wild Women" by Tim Spencer, Copyright 1947 by Tim Spencer Music Inc., Copyright Renewed, Assigned to Unichappell Music Inc. (Rightsong Music, Publisher); "Hey Good Lookin' " by Hank Williams, Copyright 1951 by Fred Rose Music, Inc., Copyright renewed 1979, assigned to Fred Rose Music, Inc., and Hiriam Music for the U.S.A. only, all rights outside the U.S.A. controlled by Fred Rose Music, Inc., International Copyright Secured, Made in U.S.A., All Rights Reserved; "If You've Got the Money (I've Got the Time)" by Lefty Frizzell and Jim Beck, Copyright 1950 by Peer International Corporation, Copyright Renewed, Used by Permission, All Rights Reserved; "A Honky-Tonk Saturday Night" by Sanger D. Shafer, Copyright 1982 by Acuff-Rose Publications, Inc., used by permission of the publisher, All Rights Reserved; "You Can't Get the Hell Out of Texas" by J. Hadley and V. Staford, recorded by George Jones on "Still the Same 'Ol Me"; "Shotgun Willie" by Willie Nelson, Copyright 1973, 1976, Willie Nelson Music, recorded on "Shotgun Willie"; "Drinkin' Them Longnecks" by Morrison, Slate, and Ryles, recorded by Roy Head on "The Many Sides of Roy Head"; "Bob Wills Is Still the King" by Waylon Jennings, recorded on "Waylon Live", 1975, RCA; "I'm a Ding Dong Daddy from Dumas" by Phil Baxter, Copyright 1928 (Renewed 1956) by Leo Feist, Inc.; "Texas Fiddle Song" by Leona Williams and Ron Williams, Shade Tree Music, Inc.

*This one is for
Erin
our honky-tonk angel*

A Word to the Wise from the author

Since this book was written for born-to-the-bone honky-tonkers who would rather dance than read, I've tried to make it a handy reference to the places where I've had fun. You can get the drift of the guide by turning to Book Two in the middle section, where you'll find photographs and maps and brief descriptions of the best honky-tonks in Texas.

I aimed to make the book easy since you know and I know that good old boys and honky-tonk angels don't read much and haven't really read nothin' since the 10th grade except maybe booze and beer labels, jukeboxes, trademarks on toilets, overdue bills, the confirmation of a horse, and dirty jokes.

One other reminder. I did my durndest to pick honky-tonks that are solid attractions, places that'll be out there on the highway long after this book has been remaindered on some bargain shelf. The title says they are the greatest. That's conjecture, my notion. You may have others. There are thousands of honky-tonks in Texas and not even a fool like me can get to them all in a lifetime. I may have missed a few, dammit.

Billy Porterfield
Old Grove Farm
Miller Grove, Texas
August, 1983

CONTENTS

Book One — We Folk

1. The Fat Mexican Polka   3
2. Car Trouble   8
3. What the Hell Is a Honky-Tonk?   13
4. Our Music   21
5. Our Red Necks   29
6. Our Womenfolk   40

Book Two — The Honky-Tonk States of Texas

7. Regions   59
8. Dallas (aka North Texas): A Strange Oasis   63
9. West Texas   71
10. The Panhandle   82
11. The Trans-Pecos   89
12. Mexican Texas   92
13. The Coast   107
14. East Texas   113
15. The Hill Country   115
16. Flab vs. Ralph   136

Book Three — The Dances

BOOK ONE

We Folk

CHAPTER 1

The Fat Mexican Polka

> I could waltz across Texas with you . . .
> "Waltz Across Texas"
> by Talmadge Tubb
> sung and recorded by
> the great Ernest Tubb

I embarrassed myself the other morning. Lynnda Bass and I were having Bloody Marys at Palms Danceland in East Dallas, listening to Texas Tequila warm up on their first medley, when this young lady walked up to the table and asked if I could do the two-step. "Yep," I said, got up and grabbed her and pumped around the floor, just the way I used to do in the Bob Wills days.

"You lunkhead," she said, calling a halt to it just as I was getting good and warm and into it, "this isn't the two-step. Let's sit down."

Well, it was A two-step. Obviously it wasn't THE two-step, the one that is the rage now, but hell, it couldn't have been as bad as she made it out to be. I mean, how many variations on the two-step can you do? But I didn't argue with her. I tend to take criticism as it's aimed, and felt cut to the quick. Puredee mortification overwhelmed me. I deposited her at her table and limped away into the morning, leaving Lynnda to shift for herself since she insisted on staying until at least noon.

It occurs to me that readers beyond the pale of Texas may think it strange a honky-tonk would open its doors for dancing and drinking during daylight hours, but down here we don't think it's as peculiar as it is handy, especially for people who work nights. The late Hondo Crouch, in a typical wry mood, once told me it was easier to sneak daylight past a rooster than it was to slip a beer past Jesus. At the time we were sitting in a cantina west of San Antonio. The sun was as fresh as the sparkle in Hondo's eyes, and he ordered another Lone Star to wash down his huevos rancheros.

That was twenty years ago. Hondo's gone, but, miraculously, I'm still kicking, and if it weren't for ladies like Lynnda and honky-tonks like Palms Danceland, which opens at 9 a.m. and closes at 5 p.m., my mornings and noons would be frozen in the rust of middle-aged atrophy. "Keep it limber," Granddaddy Harrell said. By "it" I presume he meant any extremity that wags and struts, and for the most part I've kept his advice, talking and dancing to beat the band.

There was a spell, some years ago, when I did drop out and sit home with my knees and ankles swollen and sore with gout. The doctors said I would never dance again, and I almost believed them. By the time I got straight, and could trust my kicks, Texas Chic had come and practically gone, leaving me hopping around on dance steps so old and dated that Lynnda suggested I ought to make sepia my favorite color in boots and hats and general disposition. I paid her little mind until finally one too many dance-hall ladies said thanks but no thanks. I will always owe the gal at Palms Danceland a favor for being so blunt. The humiliation forced me to reconnoiter.

The next day I asked my daughter Erin to look at my two-step and tell me what was wrong with it, in the light of today's style. I turned on the country radio and did a little number with her and she giggled.

"Dad," she said, "you're doing the Fat Mexican Polka."

"Lordy, Lordy, woman," I said. "What are you talking about? This ain't a cantina polka I'm executing, but the plain old Anglo-Celtic country two-step I learned at my daddy's knees."

"Well," she said, "whatever, it isn't right. I mean in terms of what people are doing today. Here, let me show you what I mean."

She took the part of the man. Erin turned sideways to me, cocked her hip and laid it into me, right between my legs, and off we went, dipping and sliding. I can't follow worth a damn, being used to leading, but I saw right away what she meant. It was two-stepping, but with a fine and sassy flair that was new to me.

"What do you call it, other than the two-step?" I said.

"Oh, C&W, something like that. Every urban cowboy's doing it. It's real cute, don't you think?"

"Oh, I declare," I said. "It's a scream. Here, practice me until I get it down."

As we were dancing, it struck me that close dancing was a throwback, something of a bother to the modern, liberated woman, and I said as much. "Doesn't it gall you to have to anticipate the man and go along with whatever he has in mind, instead of setting the pace yourself?"

Erin laughed. "Dad," she said, "just dance. Shut up and dance."

"Naw," I went on, "I'm serious. Here. Let's try it. You lead and I'll follow."

It didn't work. Funny thing. Since she came into puberty with a green-eyed blond-haired vengeance, Erin has gone out of her way to do the opposite of what I tell her. It's taken a few years, but I'm finally getting it into my noggin that she wants to lead her own life. It was hard to swallow at first, but now I see it as an admirable if damn fool thing on her part, because if she'd let me, I'd run it into the ground telling her how the cow eats the cabbage.

Still, when it comes to dancing, she'd rather follow than lead. I'll take that, figuring it's all I can get. But it isn't a sop. Plainly, it's what she prefers. But I wonder if it'll hold. Now that women can have babies without men, and now that men can have babies without women, I wonder what the two-step will be in the future. It's something to think about. But I wasn't up to it. Just conquering the C&W two-step was about the extent of my ambition right then, that and getting my 1955 Buick in good running order.

I come from a long line of dancers. My maternal grandfather, a short, squat blacksmith named Daddy Harrell, was the king of country dancing on both sides of the Red River. You get up around Ardmore and Madill and like as not some old coot will recall his Crosstown Strut, and if the music's right and the old knee is spry, you might get a demonstration.

It was indescribable, Papa Harrell's Crosstown Strut. Uncle Herschel and Aunt Marguerite said that from behind it looked like two pigs fighting in a tow sack, which was only a third of it. You had to see it to believe it. They always said that. I never saw it myself, since he was off hoboing on the railroad when I came along. My Aunt Cora and my Aunt Maude, who were the matriarchs of the clan after Granny died and fine Christian women, said the Crosstown Strut was lowdown dirty, obscene, and anytime they were around Daddy Harrell and anyone so much as whistled a tune, they'd gather up their skirts and leave, claiming no kin to him since they were from the other side of the family.

Everything was music to Papa. A mule could bray and he'd mistake it for a melody. The wind whistling through the pines threw him into a rhapsody. When Aunt Esther sang at Mama Harrell's funeral, it was all they could do to hold Daddy Harrell down and keep him from dancing over his wife's open coffin. He cried, "They who hear not the music, think the dancers mad!" Then he sat down and let the preacher finish. He meant no disrespect. It was a compliment to Mama Harrell, and sad when you think about it. In all their years together, they never danced. She played the mandolin and sang through her nose as pretty as you please, but she couldn't dance, was terribly self-conscious about it, and spent all her Saturday nights as a wallflower watching Papa Harrell prance with the prettiest women in the county.

The point is the dance which had been passed down in the blood was no longer first nature to me. Erin was right. It turned out I was confusing the Fat Mexican Polka with my old country two-step. This was laid on me by my new wife, Nanette, who came out of the dance halls of Houston. So she and Erin went into cahoots to turn me around. It took some doing. The Fat Mexican was so deeply a part of me . . . well, I must tell you about it.

* * *

The only way to get to Cibolo from Seguin is to go through Nolte, Blumberg Spur, Hilda, McQueeney and Marion. I didn't mind Nolte, Blumberg Spur, Hilda and McQueeney, but I hated the thought of driving through Marion.

Marion herself is not offensive. She's a pleasant little place on the Guadalupe County map — hardly makes much of a dent in the bumper of your mind. But I was in a hurry and I knew I could not just pass through Marion. It would be about noon, and a cloudy scent of jalapeno frijoles and polecat tamales would waft up from a kitchen on Canyon Pond, cross the mesquite and cactus and hang there over the road to fog its flavors onto my windshield and insinuate its aromas into the seams of the car and into my very nose.

I would have no choice but to stop, back up a bit, turn left at the dirt road, and bump down around the pond and up to the door of the Fat Mexican Cafe. The place was named after its proprietor and sole employee, Gloria, who every day weighed more than she had the day before but could dance the lightest feet off.

I mention dance right off because Gloria would serve no mouth unless it had feet for dancing, feet that were ready to lead Gloria 'round the floor to the Fat Mexican Polkas which played on the Fat Mexican jukebox. The better you danced, the bigger servings you got.

The fare at the Fat Mexican never varied. You had peppery beans on one side of the plate, a savory stack of tamales on the other, and in the middle a clove or two of garlic peeled and dipped in chile sauce and laid upon a bed of hot flour tortillas. Such a meal took time to eat because it was hot as in temperature, hot as in spice, and so provocative that you wanted more — a second helping and maybe a third — before you put your fork down and finished off a last beer. By this time most mortal men were in no shape to drive on to wherever they were going, so what you did was waddle outside, stretch out on the long porch with the dogs and cats and chickens, and nap in the elements until your digestion would let you continue down the road.

We regular customers always thought Gloria would get in trouble with the authorities over her tamales. She advertised them on a single sign outside and on the menu as polecat tamales, which meant to most readers that the spicy meat that went into the roll was skunk. Needless to say, this drove away more customers than ever dared enter. But once past that bluff, the hearty diner discovered that Gloria loved to tease, that all she was serving in the tamales were plain old domestic and stray cats and nothing so hideous and unappetizing as *zorillo*.

But the thing that led to Gloria's downfall, and her demise as a restaurateur, was her violation of certain customers' civil rights. Her problem was that she always reserved the right to refuse service to anyone, namely slackers on the dancefloor. In effect, what she ran was a private club and the key was that you had to dance and drink beer with her before eating. You'd be surprised. As great a gal and fine a dancer as she was, some guys were put off, even offended, and they refused to pay their dues, so to speak. Out they went and that was that. *"No bailar, no comer."* Not to dance is not to eat. Simple as that.

But it was two women's libbers from Jersey who did Gloria in. How they got off the interstate to find the Fat Mexican we will never know. They showed up late one afternoon and ordered the plate lunch, and when Gloria said she couldn't serve them, they wanted to know why. Gloria explained, in a ladylike and logical way, that she couldn't serve anyone unless they danced with her, and since they were ladies and she was a lady, dancing together was impossible, or at least not any fun, and maybe they had better go. But the women wouldn't budge. They said they were hungry, and wouldn't at all mind dancing for some beans. Besides, they added, it wasn't odd to see women dancing together, nor, for that matter, men, where they came from.

"Not out here," Gloria said, and threw them out.

They returned through lawyers and gave Gloria hell. The feds got tough with her, and Gloria finally threw up her hands, chased off her cats and customers, and closed the doors. Marion was never the same, and, of course, there was never any gold in Cibolo once you got there.

That was my training in the Fat Mexican Polka. It served me well for years, and it cost Nanette and Erin, with a little red-headed help from Lynnda, a small fortune in honky-tonk cover charges and beer to get it out of me. Now, refortified and up-to-date, we started hitting the new high spots like Billy Bob's Texas in Fort Worth. Once in a while I would write about it my column in the *Dallas Times Herald*. This led J. Nelson Black of Taylor Publishing Company to my door with a handsome proposition. Why didn't I go ahead and do a book on the honky-tonks of Texas?

"That's a lot of travel, Jim. Texas is a big state."

"Your old bones not up to it?"

"Bones are fine. It's my Buick. I don't know if she's got that much wind left in her. But we'll give it a whirl."

So off we went.

CHAPTER 2

Car Trouble

> Are you chure you wan' to feex eet, amigo? I doan know what to say, man. All I can say for chure is that theese car has seen eet's day, like you and me, man, that's for damn chure. Watch out, Pepe! Doan touch eet so hard. Eet might fall apart. What can I say, amigo? Maybe yes, maybe no. Come back tomorrow.
> — *Lopez of Brackettville*

Ma used to say you could always tell a trashy family by the number of scroungy dogs and useless old cars in the yard. Two dogs were okay, and so were two vehicles — as long as one had all four tires inflated and a fair-to-middling chance of starting on a cold morning. Anything else over that was, in Mother's eyes, definitely hicksville. She said this often, and with passion if not much effect, since we boys went on collecting every stray dog and rusty car part we came across and dumping them on the front porch. Mother went to her grave thinking that journalism and the big city would act as a refinement on me. Foolish woman. She knew nothing of this trade and never would have guessed it would make me even seedier.

Take last winter at my place in East Texas.

First, there was the matter of the dogs. We started out with one, a male cocker spaniel, and that was to be it. But then my daughter began coming out with her male schnauzer, one of those miniature, snappy yelps, and along behind came her friend, Graham, with his German shepherd pup, a female of amazing patience. Then a friend (or foe) deposited on our doorstep a mongrel waif with a broken forepaw. If we didn't take him in, a vet would have to put him to sleep. He was part collie and shepherd, with big brown eyes that told a tragic tale of abuse and abandonment. Then one morning this comically grotesque thing showed up all on his own. He was a weenie of a mutt, low, long and no-legged and sharp-faced like a dachshund, but crossed with enough bull terrier to give him big feet and a short, thick coat of white with black spots. Or was it black with white spots? Whatever, the dog was a sight, pathetic really, a freak. His legs were flippers with oversized toes, and I thought if he stood upright he would waddle like a penguin. The other thing

I thought was that he was persistent. I did everything short of murder to drive him away, but he would not leave and that was that. Yes, Mother, raise up from your grave and count them. And be patient. The cars are coming.

It isn't just the mangy hides, crossed eyes and greedy mouths playing among the tires, towheads and pine cones that make me a throwback to Appalachian rednecks. It is the way I waste my time simply trying to function on the most basic level. Like getting up on a cold morning and having the car start so I can go to work. It is never my fault when something goes wrong. This is a dead giveaway to the redneck character. Them are always to blame, never us'un. Them idiots in Detroit who make plastic cars. Them morons in Washington and the infernal revenue. Them is simply the fates, in whatever guise, which are always ill-disposed and out to get you. And they do. They get you every time. They'll kick you when you're so down you're almost mud. And they'll come back and kick you just when you've pulled yourself up and think maybe you're getting ahead and that everything's going to be fine, which, of course, it isn't, ever. Ma called them the wraiths, said they came with being low-class.

The wraiths started on me when Nanette and I sat down to plan our travels. We would have to do it on weekends, since the *Herald* keeps me hopping throughout the week. We would have to get someone to feed the dogs and we would have to get the cars in good running order. The family heirloom, the rusty, baby blue over rusty, dirty diaper-white 1955 Buick Special, had been roosting in the barn with the chickens for years. It had been a good road car when Eisenhower was president, and I told Nanette that if we ever got it going I would have more confidence in it than her 1980 Oldsmobile diesel.

"I don't know," she said. "The Oldsmobile is not exactly state-of-the-art diesel, but God, Billy, it looks to me like that old Buick makes a better chicken coop than it does a car. Are you sure you want to waltz across Texas in a contraption like that?"

Since Nanette was only born in 1959, I had to set her straight. I told her that the Buick was good and heavy and solid, like the 1950's, that there was not a piece of plastic on it and that it still had the original everythings, a bit faded and chipped, yes, but somehow still almost elegant.

I told her how I liked the wide, deep, bench seats which smelled of banana-haired girls, prom corsages, Teen Town and Johnny Ray and 100-mile-an-hour beer busts and moonings between Goliad and Corpus Christi when her father, and I, yes, and her mother were one and twenty. I told her I liked the way I had to sit on a telephone book to see over the steering wheel, which was steamboat wide and high and hard to turn. I liked the smooth tick of the V-8 engine, the sonic mesh of the Dynaflow transmission and the amazing fact that the lumbering land whale got 22 miles a gallon on the highway with poor regular gasoline.

It was an automobile so sturdy and sure in its chassis that fender benders would not blemish the shine and contour of its massive bumpers, fore and aft. The metal skin of the body was thick, its paint so hard that West Texas hailstones were bouquets thrown by the gods, that beneath all that chicken shit and barn dust was a shining jewel of the road. In short, it was everything that America used to be not only in its cars but in its six-ounce Cokes, its Maytags, its Singers, its Triple Crown winners, movie stars and presidents. It had staying power over the long haul. This Buick had no flash-in-the-pan, built-in-obsolescence buttons to go off beeping and blinking the day after you made your last installment payment. Nobody had to say, "Wouldn't you really rather have a Buick?" They built the mother to run for 500,000 miles and then be hauled off to the junkyard to be melted down into a tank, which was its next of kin.

When the Buick was made were the days when the chairman of GM was secretary of defense, and what was good for GM was good for the country. Anyway, this is what I had in mind retrieving with the Buick. Something of my youth, yes, but also a sense of stability in the running of the country and the economy as well as an automobile. It's funny how we forget the lousy things, like Teller and McCarthy, polio and castor oil, Korea, Jim Crow and the bus drivers in Montgomery. Poor Nanette. She subsided and said, okay, maybe so.

"Look," I said. "I know the Buick is old and worn, if not from mileage so much as inactivity and sitting on its heavy haunches all these years. I figure a thousand bucks will bring it back to as close to perfect as it's ever been. How about it? I can borrow the money from the credit union."

"Darlin'," she said. "I've got to believe in rejuvenation or I wouldn't have married you. Go ahead, reclaim your precious keepsake. I'll make ends meet as best I can."

"Great! I'll take it to Lopez's garage in Kaufman this weekend. He ought to have her in good shape in a couple of weeks."

And I was almost right. Senor Lopez had it in his garage for four months. There was a lot to be done, and only a saint like Lopez would have taken it on. The most difficult job was not fixing it but finding the parts. A car that sits that long loses the cartilage and cushion between its bones. Its pipes rust and it loses its breath and its get-up-and-go. Lopez kept finding one thing after another that needed replacing.

None of these thingamajigs were easily replaced. We ran ourselves ragged looking for parts, since GM stopped making them for my car when I still had hair on top of my head. I found myself tramping through many a rock midden of old car culture, dealing with characters who were as ornery as their junkyard dogs. They weren't much help to me with my car, but I did get a line on some of your basic killer honky-tonks, none of which I'll mention out of a sense of responsibility for my fellow man.

At last I discovered B. S. Wisniewski, Inc., Milwaukee's oldest discount house and dealer in home appliances and car parts. All I had to do was phone Wisniewski and ask for Paul, their auto archaeologist, and say, "Paul, this is

Porterfield in Texas. Do you have coil springs and shocks for my 1955 Buick Special?"

"If I don't, I can," Paul would say.

He would quote me prices. "That'll be $39.95 for two front shocks, $140.00 for two rear shocks, and $20.00 for the rear links. I'll throw in the coil springs free and give you a $40.00 refund on your old rear shocks."

Senor Lopez put them in as fast as Paul could send them — gaskets for a tuned-up engine, new belts, new wiring, new hoses and heater ducts, seals for the transmission, etc.

In the meantime, I was having hell getting to work and generally peevish and half off the wall because time was a'wasting on the honky-tonk book. It was the wraiths again.

They started on me one morning after a slight freeze. I got up to discover that the Oldsmobile diesel sedan would not go. Oh, for a few hundred dollars you could buy an automatic heating unit that would help it start when it was cold, but it wasn't standard equipment.

I got my daughter to come and drive me over to her brother's house. Since he was away at college, his 1973 Volkswagen sat in the garage. I would drive the bug timorously. It wears its nine front-end and rear-end collisions like battle trophies. We went forth in Erin's 1980 Renault, which I am paying for but which has no safety inspection sticker or current license plate because I always forget to mail her the forms.

As I drove her brother's crumpled bug toward the *Times Herald*, I discovered it had only the breath of a brake. Somehow I made it to Griffin and Pacific, warned Joe, the parking lot boss, and went up and took seven hours to write one chicken little column.

Although I made it home, the wraiths were still with me, waiting. By Friday night I was at the place in East Texas, sending a thin blue line of hackberry smoke up the stove pipe and looking forward to two days of country idyll. The diesel was running again (the weather had warmed), which meant that Saturday Nanette would drop me off at Lopez's garage to pick up, at long last, the Buick. Then we would be ready to hit the road in search of the best honky-tonks in Texas.

"Put some gas in it," Lopez warned. "You only got about seven miles worth."

"I can make it to Terrell," I said. "I'll gas up there."

My tank went dry the other side of Cartwright, halfway to Terrell. I didn't realize how cold it had turned until I got out and started walking. My hat blew off and floated away in a creek. Now there was nothing covering my bean but the frizz around the edges. I thought my ears would freeze off. An independent trucker picked me up and cussed President Reagan all the way to the gas station in Terrell. The people at the gas station wouldn't rent me a portable gas can, so I had to walk six blocks to an auto parts store and buy one. I walked a half mile to another gas station, got me a gallon, and headed down the road again. A welder picked me up after about 30 minutes and tried to save my soul for Christ before he dropped me at the Buick.

I emptied the gallon in the Buick, but ran the battery down trying to get the gas up that cold line from the tank to the carburetor. I hitchhiked back into Terrell, hired the service station fellow to drive me out and give the Buick a boost. You must understand that in all this travail I felt lucky because I had just gotten paid by the *Herald* and felt flush. Usually I would have been up the creek without a paddle. Anyway, as I humped along toward town for a fillup, I cursed the fates and wondered what Ronald Reagan was doing at that very moment. *My* sole intent was to get past crusty places like Eula, Brim and Tona without my car giving out. *His* was to make history, damn his hide.

I tanked up in Terrell, and by the time I reached the Sabine River in Hunt County, I allowed myself to think that I was ahead and that everything was going to be all right.

No such luck. On a hill above the river, I ran over one of the shortest nails on record, but because my treads were so thin, it deflated one of the front tires. Of course, the spare was flat. And no, I had nothing to fix it. A man named Red Purcell picked me up in his red pickup and took me to a bait stand which had a gas pump and a patch man, for which I will ever be grateful.

As I drove into my place in the woods, the hood of the Buick flew up in my face, cracking the windshield, and I almost ran over that crippled pup.

"The Buick still isn't ready," I confessed to Nanette.

"Well, don't sit around and moan about it," she said. "You can go ahead and start writing on the book anyway."

"What can I say? Some of these joints I haven't been to in years."

"We'll get to them, Billy. In the meantime, why don't you sit down at the typewriter and tell us what the hell honky-tonks are? There are people in Jersey probably who've never heard of them. You know, tell about the music and the kind of people who inspire it, the folks you grew up with and all. Then, we and the reader can hit the road with more in mind than just a road map to guide us."

It was, at least, a start. The day I bought a new battery and tires for the Buick, I picked up a fresh ribbon for my old Underwood. And I began.

CHAPTER 3

What the Hell Is a Honky-Tonk?

> I went to a dance
> Wore out my shoes,
> Woke up this morning wishin'
> I could lose this jumpin'
> Honky-Tonk Blues,
> This weary Honky-Tonk Blues.
> Lord, I'm sufferin' with the
> Honky-Tonk Blues.
>
> "Honky-Tonk Blues"
> by Hank Williams

Need I say the Fat Mexican Cafe was not a honky-tonk? Probably. With so many Yankees settling in among us, and so many of our own young becoming citified and conned by Texas Chic, it won't hurt to define our terms. There's no sense in going to a dictionary for help. Can you imagine a Yale man with a taste for philology actually coming to grips with a colloquialism like honky-tonk? Noah Webster and his successors can't do it. I've got half a dozen dictionaries and they all throw in the towel by dismissing a honky-tonk as a cheap, noisy saloon or dance hall. Granted, there's some truth in the description, but not enough to make you think that any of the lexicographers ever set foot in such a place. Harold Wentworth and Stuart Berg Flexner do no better in their *Dictionary of American Slang.*

Still, I thought I had to seek out some scholarly authority to give this book more weight than I could muster with my own experiences in lowdown dives. It dawned on me that the expert I should have gone to in the first place is Dr. James Ward Lee, the professor of honky-tonks at North Texas State University in Denton. The fact that Jim teaches in the English department at North Texas and has written five books of high literary quality isn't nearly as important for our purposes as his accomplishments in the folk culture field. Jim was born a folk himself, and knows more about rednecks and honky-tonks than any educated man I know. This means he has to run a respectable third behind louts like Larry L. King and me. He has both hybrid vigor and a pedigree.

What Jim says is that no one knows for sure the origin of the term, honky-tonk. In his essay, "The Glamor of the Gay Night Life: The Classic Honky-Tonk," which appeared in a 1982 publication of the Texas Folklore Society, Jim writes that "Perhaps in the earliest use of the term, honky-tonk described Negro jazz clubs, for there is a song, 'Honky-Tonky Town,' which tells of a place 'underneath the ground' with 'singing waiters, singing syncopaters' who are 'dancing to piano played by Mr. Brown.' Mr. Brown plays piano 'queer; he only plays by ear.' The implications of the song are that ragtime or jazz is the music, that Mr. Brown is what used to be called a man of color, and that the establishment — Honky-Tonky Town — is operating on the fringes of the law."

Well, you can play around with the front part of the term. Honk means to toot raucously, to have a little fun raising hell, and that fits. And, in black slang, a honky is a white man. And that works too, since Jim Lee and anybody with a little sun on his neck will tell you that at least since the 1930's honky-tonks have been associated almost exclusively with poor Southern whites. As Dr. Lee puts it, "The honky-tonk is the working man's club; his haven of rest and recreation, his place to repair — to use (abuse?) the word in two of its best senses." But what of tonk? Your guess is as good as ours. It remains a mystery.

But enough of this word-fencing. The honky-tonk has been a fiddling fact along the road of Southern life for well over half a century, its parking lot full of cars and pickups, its dance floor packed with dancers and its bar dispensing beer, and maybe booze, long after the cows have come home.

How can you say when a thing begins or ends? Maybe it began with the harvest dances, the roundup shindigs, and it remained — this habit of partying after work — even as the work and the people themselves changed.

In his book, *Country Music, U.S.A.*, Bill C. Malone writes that "Many of the security patterns of an older rural existence seemed to be decaying. The country person in the increased mobility of the decades following 1930 experienced the breakup of home, family and church relationships. As Alan Lomax has said, the rural Southerner was the last to know 'the sorrows of divorce and unstable love affairs, and to discover the loneliness of a society in which the village, the clan and the family were in dissolution.' His songs reflected the changing status . . .

"The factors which produced new forms and styles within country music were in evidence all over the South. It was in Texas, however, that conditions proved to be most fertile for new developments. Since the thirties Texas had contributed many of the most spectacular stars to country music, and most of them received their basic musical training in a common school. This was a social institution, springing up in the chaotic ferment of the depressions, designed for the needs of rural dwellers: the honky-tonk. Saloons and taverns, of course, were not new to the American scene, but they assumed a new significance in the thirties. The Texas oil boom created a number of frontier-like areas where wide-open taverns, selling illegal liquor, catered to the desires of oil workers. With the repeal of prohibition in 1933 the taverns were given a confirmed status. These taverns usually were situated on the outskirts of town for a variety of reasons. In this location tax rates were lower, police supervision was apt to be more lax, and it was relatively easy for both city and rural dwellers to reach the place. In Texas, with some counties 'dry' and others 'wet,' the county-line tavern developed. These wayside taverns were sometimes only small, dingy bars, but quite often contained a dancefloor. Here, farmers, laborers, truck drivers, and displaced rural dwellers gathered to relax and drink beer or to work off their frustrations (or add to them) by an occasional round of merriment or 'hell-raising.' Many of the honky-tonks, particularly in Texas' German communities, were family affairs where everyone could gather for merriment, and where special places were set aside for the children."

That pretty well says it, in a sociological kind of way.

In his paean to honky-tonks, Professor Lee writes that "The real honky-tonk — even after all these years — is set up on the skirts of a town. Out where men are men, women are double breasted, and property values have been ruined by junkyards, parts houses, and pawn shops. Out where the minorities dwell. Out where the noble '55 Chevy sits regally atop concrete blocks in the front yard. In short, out on those edges of towns and cities where life is real and life is earnest and the bank account is but an empty dream. Or if not in town, the classic place may be out alongside the ubiquitous frontage road . . ."

Amen, brother, amen. The way Jim describes the classic honky-tonk is exactly the way I remember Rob's Place in Robstown. It was not the first honky-tonk I was ever in, but it became, in 1940 when I was eight, the capitol of my honky-tonk heart, the place where Nashville radio WSM's Grand Ole Opry took on a local reality, for it was there that the great country music stars came, the very singers and players you heard on the old Magnavox in the living room at home. It was there that I first saw in the flesh Bob Wills and his Texas Playboys, and, yes, the daddy of honky-tonk music, Ernest Tubb. We had heard Tubb on KONO out of San Antonio, and later on KGKO in Fort Worth. When he sold beer he was the Texas Troubadour, and when he sold flour he was the Gold Chain Troubadour, and I tell you the night he came to play at Rob's Place, sporting Jimmie Rodgers' $2000 guitar and promoting his first record for RCA — the sides were "I'll Get Along Somehow" and "Blue-Eyed Elaine" — we and everybody within 50 miles were there with our hearts in our throats. Uncle Earl and Aunt Arbie drove over from Corpus Christi, and I remember asking Arbie if it was disrespectful to get up and dance when a star like Ernest Tubb was singing.

"No honey, he wants us to," she said, and grabbed me up to glide around the floor as if I were a real man.

Robstown was about 40 miles west of Corpus and the coast, once a part of the Driscoll Ranch and named after that family's *patron*, Robert. A flat of cactus and mesquite, the area had been transformed by farmers into a great savannah of grain and cotton. Then oil had been discovered, and that had brought the likes of us and the honky-tonks, of which Rob's Place was the favorite. I don't know if a Rob was the proprietor, or if the name of the place was a play on the name of the town. We were just oil patch people. We didn't walk into a dance hall and introduce ourselves to the management. We just put on our talc and hair oil, bought a bottle of hootch (which we kept hidden in the car, requiring many trips back and forth between the dancing and the drinking), paid the cover, and enjoyed ourselves. Rob's Place itself was a long, low rectangle of a building, white slapboard, which faced U.S. 77 south of town. The club backed into a field of black gumbo, which in the spring and summer was high with milo maize and in the winter was a dangerous bog if Daddy had had a little too much beer and didn't keep the car on the caliche.

As you entered, the front part of the building had a bar on the right side and on the left, tables and chairs and a couple of pool tables and marble machines and a shuffleboard. If you were hungry, you could get cold cuts and hot links at the bar, which only served beer and pop. If you wanted to dance, you had to walk through a gate in a little wooden fence that cut off the dancefloor from the front. During the day there was no cover and you could dance to the jukebox as long as you had the nickels and quarters. At night if the house band was playing you paid a dollar to get in and had your hand stamped with magic ink so you could come and go without having to pay over again. On special weekends, when a big-name outfit was playing, the cover was doubled and you had to arrive early to get a table around the dancefloor. If you were called to dance or pee, you always left a member of your party to hold down your place and watch the purses.

The toilets may have been inside or outside. It didn't matter. They were always filthy. It didn't matter to us men, but it must've been a mess for the ladies.

The accommodations were always tawdry, but hell, so were we and our dreams. Our lives were plain enough, or had been before we left the farms and moved up and down the highways getting closer to the cities and their enticing ways. We began to try to make things fancier than they were and ended up making them trashy. Only we didn't know it. We had never heard the word *kitsch* (it wasn't coined yet, but we wouldn't have known it anyway). Mother went right on gluing sequins onto the new plastic bottles Johnson & Johnson was using for its baby oil. Why not? Our greatest country music stars wore shiny scales on everything, even their guitars. My cousin Crystal Ball wasn't named that for nothing. Her parents may never have seen a real crystal ball, but they had danced under many a glittering glass-and-plastic revolving ball. But more about Crystal Ball and our sense of taste later. The point is that honky-tonks were cheap places frequented by low-class (which is not a crime) customers. They were not particularly dangerous places, although some were. If a fight broke out, the best bet was to keep dancing. The tone of a place depended more on the management than the customers. You can take any class of people and find among them a slice of life and character which runs the gamut from good to bad, and certainly this was true, *is* true, for honky-tonk folk.

The curious thing about dance halls I've noticed is how much raunchier they get the closer they are to towns and cities. It still holds if you don't count the new, urban cowboy palaces where dress codes and manners are strictly enforced. The basic country dance hall was as American Gothic plain as the prairie house and the prairie church. A community center, it was a broad expanse of wooden floor with a roof on it and hinged board flaps around it which opened on hot nights to let in the smell of new-mown hay. There was a rude bar against one wall, hardly any signs or advertisements or decorations, since the place was only open on weekends and did not represent the interest of any single proprietor so much as it stood for the whole community and its recreation.

There are still some of the old halls left, especially in Central and South Texas, and they remain my favorites over the honky-tonks in town. Most of them have passed into private ownership now, and are run on a more sophisticated and profitable basis, which means they are evolving into honky-tonks. But still, there's enough of the rural in the air and in the warp and woof of country faces and bodies that it seems like home. There is a lack of affectation in country dance halls like Floore's at Helotes that is absolutely anachronistic and wonderful.

In the country halls people dress as they please and dance as they please. This is how I was raised. Yes, in a group dance, such as the schottische, there was a set way to move your feet, but when you latched onto your partner it was let 'er rip in any way you felt or were inclined by idiosyncrasy or whatever it was that made you dance the way you did. We weren't self-conscious or as conscious of what somebody else was doing. Hell, I'd go so far as to say that we weren't conscious at all, except that we were keenly aware of having a good time. This kind of eccentric oblivion (you go your way and I'll go mine) was so strong in the country halls and honky-tonks of my youth that today I find it damned nigh stifling to go to some new C & W spot in the city and find everybody dancing the same way, or trying to. Them that don't dance sit around and admire them that dance the same as everyone else only better. There's something chilling about the young kickers' desire to fit in, to wear the right label jeans and boots, the feather band in the hat, and to do the two-step in the approved way. But then, as you remember from the first chapter of this odyssey, I too suffered from a fear of being out-of-step, so I can't make too much of this. I've lived and worked too long in the cities, that's my problem.

The closer revelers get to town, the more goop they put on their faces and bodies and the more goop and nonsense they give one another. It not only happens to people, it happens to the places they frequent. Wooden tables and benches have to be covered up with Naugahyde or vinyl. Windows have to be insulated to keep in the noise. Lights come on, but shaded with color and mood. Voices and instruments are softened with filters to hide the blemishes and then the ideal is magnified out of all proportion. The price of beer and whiskey goes up. Pool tables and shuffleboard games are joined by pinball machines, video games and mechanical bulls. The singer for the house band starts to make hit records and people from all over pour in. A Hollywood producer decides to make a film there and it becomes world famous. The beautiful people come, duded up in Cutter Bill outfits and Gucci boots. The joint is so *in* it becomes a conglomerate of enterprises, hawking T-shirts, souvenirs and even sponsoring a rodeo and publishing its own house organ. Of course, I'm describing Gilley's in Pasadena, which Jim Lee doesn't think is a honky-tonk.

He writes: "All sorts of pseudo-honky-tonks now exist, but the real thing retains the old-time characteristics. Places like Gilley's in Pasadena, Texas with its mechanical bull, and the newly opened Billy Bob's Texas with its capacity of 6,000 hardly qualify as honky-tonks. Nor do all the so-called C&W discos, which are usually failed rock and roll places or singles bars for secretaries and shoe clerks who want to play cosmic cowboy or cosmic cowgirl — or should it be cosmic cowperson?"

I agree with Lee about the discos, but not about Gilley's and Billy Bob's. Gilley's is entire unto itself, like no other. But, curiously, its fame has obscured its everynight character, which it has had for years before John Travolta set a stagy foot in the stirrup of the bucking bull. Gilley's was an edge-of-the-big-city honky-tonk for South Houston factory workers fresh from the sticks, as rough and authentically vulgar as you would want, and it is still that when the tourists aren't around. I love the damn place. Not to call Gilley's a honky-tonk is to say that the King Ranch is no longer the real thing because they don't allow the bulls to sock it to the cows anymore. It is more efficient and profitable to have an AI technician — an artificial inseminator — to send the frozen seed home with rubber gloves. Times and ways change. At least at Gilley's, like at any other honky-tonk, girls get danced good and laid later.

It's true that since the urban cowboy craze a lot of C&W dance halls have come, and now many are going as the faddists trade in their boots and hats for something else. But the ones that are dying existed only for the fashion. Once the moment was gone, they were gone. Good riddance. There are enough true honky-tonkers to keep the solid places thriving. Billy Bob's came on the crest of a craze, but because of its city — Fort Worth — and its location — the old stockyards — I think it's here to stay in its high, wide and handsome way. If any people have a right to play cowboy, it's the folks in Cowtown.

Some of you readers may have noticed how, in the space of a few pages, the honky-tonk has headed out of the rural South of farmers and turned toward the urban West of questionable cowboys. Well, in history it took only a little longer for the roadhouses to reach the ranch country. We laid roads fast in Texas, and it was nothing, is still nothing, for a ranchhand to drive 70 miles to a Saturday night dance.

When you think about it, the urban cowboys are not the first to ride off into a day-glo glittered West. Some of us have been playing cowboys and Indians since Little Big Horn. Even Sitting Bull, the Sioux chief who did Custer in, turned theatrical and joined Buffalo Bill's Wild West Show to reenact The Last Stand for audiences across the land. It was the time of the great cattle drives, when 40,000 drovers and 300,000 saddle horses were going up the trails to market behind 10 million cows. Even as the real cowboy worked the range, we were transforming him into our hearts' desire, pretending there was a little of him in each of us. We read Western magazines and Western novels, went to rodeos and Western movies, sang cowboy songs and tried to talk his lingo.

Larry McMurtry has noted that as a craft, cowboying has only existed for about 120 years, and has been in decline for at least half that time and has never involved very many people. "Yet," he says, "its potency in American myth is practically unrivaled."

In McMurtry's introduction to "Panhandle Cowboy," written by Perryton cowpoke John Erickson, McMurtry supposes that "Part of this potency can be explained by the fact that it is a pastoral craft — in the increasingly suburbanized American environment even to think about the pastoral brings a kind of uplift. But if there can be said to be a core element in cowboying, that element is probably independence. In point of fact, as John Erickson repeatedly makes clear, cowboys depend on a good many things besides themselves — on horses, neighbors, and luck, to name only three — but even so, and despite the fact that they are ultimately somebody's employee, the practice of their craft allows them a far greater sense of independence than most Americans now feel. It is in the joining of a deep and rhythmic pastoralism with a challenging and sustaining independence that the resonance of the cowboy myth resides."

When the redneck tenant farmers and the tanned cowboys got together in the dance halls on the outskirts of town, they shared this sense of rugged individualism. Both were bound to landowners for their livelihood. Neither one had a pot to piss in. It was in this Catch 22, this tension between the indentured and the free, that they became true existentialists. Of course, if you told one of them that, he would have thought you were cussing him and would have socked you in the eye. Using fancy words in a honky-tonk is almost as bad as dancing with another man. You do it only once.

The curiosity for me is the character and costume change the mythical cowboy has undergone in the popular guise.

The old romanticism had him a gentle knight, a shepherd, repulsed by the airs of civilized society and the press of technology, indifferent to arms and aggression, content to ride herd on his boss's cattle. He was so shy the only thing he would kiss was his horse.

But then we put a six-shooter in his hand and made him a killer and an outlaw.

Then we started to dude him up with rhinestones, and he became a drugstore cowboy, a singing cowboy, and we went through Gene Autry and Roy Rogers and now Willie Nelson and Waylon Jennings. Before, cowboys hadn't done all that well with women, but Gene and Roy began to get the girls in a scrubbed and decorous kind of way. Willie and Waylon changed that, or rather they symbolize the change. The cowboy had taken to the road, not the range, and he hung out at roadhouses and honky-tonks with rednecks. He lived for faster horses, older whiskey, young women and more money. It took only a little twist, a turn from the rural good ole boy to the city slicker, to come up with Mickey Gilley and John Travolta and the urban kickers. In between all this, the cowboy was also a showboat athlete and fashion-plate, personified in Larry Mahan.

Out on the ranches, there were transformations. After Bet-A-Million Gates wrapped the ranches in barbed wire, the cowboy was fenced in. If he wasn't willing to stay put and mend fences, bale hay and drive a tractor, he wasn't worth hiring. You found ranchers correcting you. "I'm a cowman, not a cowboy." The former implied manful responsibility and no nonsense — a manager, a businessman in boots and gabardine — the latter immaturity and a romantic nature — the shiftless drifter.

It wasn't long before this stolid cowman was corrupted and profaned. He found oil on his place and got filthy rich. Enter the wheeler-dealers, the cattlemen with oil royalties, the oilmen with cows. Thus was born the new rich, the vulgar rich, the fat and sassy barbarians who loved to put on a show at Neiman's. The lean and laconic knight of the saddle was lost in the fat and loud braggart in a Cadillac. And now we say howdy to J.R. and the Ewings out at suburban South Fork.

So you see, the cowboy has been a transmutation so long, an incredibly enduring hallucination, that I tend to marvel at the latest wrinkle rather than feel offense. After all, I'm one of the poseurs myself. So Jim Lee's cosmic cowpersons around counterfeit campfires, breathing burning grass and drinking longnecks, listening to the lowing of Darrell Royal's Longhorns, they amuse more than bewilder. Certainly Gilley's and Billy Bob's and Austin City Limits are the right settings for the crossbreeding of country and city strains, at long last consummated in music. It isn't bad really, the rhinestone imitation. I do it myself, affecting tight jeans, Charlie Dunn boots, a macho moustache and three mares. It flatters the past and those men we want for our models. If our imitation is sentimental and inaccurate, it is because something has been lost in the translation. And that's Jim Lee's lament when it comes to honky-tonks. We are what we were, but not quite.

CHAPTER 4

Our Music

"The moods which seem particularly American to me are the noisy ribaldry, the sadness, a groping earnestness..."

— *Roy Harris, composer*
1898-1980

With the exception of a local polka band who might make a record or two, most of the music we heard at home and in the honky-tonks and cafes was what we called hillbilly. At first it had been mountain music, as sweet and pure as the harvest moon and that dear old mother and silver-haired daddy of mine. It was sentimental and close to home and hearth, and the church, and nobody could sing it through their blessed noses better than the Carter family. But as Lomax and Malone say, say, the times and the circumstances changed. We were no longer removed from the rest of the country by distance and bad roads and the insularity of country ways and traditions. It is a law of civilization that cities devour villages. And corrupt country youths. A lifetime of hymns couldn't hold us. And little Jimmie Rodgers, the blue yodeler from Meridian, Mississippi, rode a fast train to early sorrow, sickness and death as he sang his way to glory. He was, perhaps, the first Southern white commercial artist to sing the blues, the first to hit the road and ride the rails, to gamble and drink in a rough and rowdy way and run off from the chain gang and sweat the T.B. which would kill him two days after his last recording. Downhome music had become hardtime music.

Larry L. King calls it the passion of the common man, and in an article in the *Texas Monthly* of August, 1976, he wrote: "... this native American art form soon came to be associated with the Great Depression — the first universal experience to be shared after the country music genre came into its own. We rootless or ruined children of the Thirties identified with the drifting hobo or a silver-haired daddy left somewhere behind. Our songs commemorated the people and places we knew: whiskey widows, sisters menaced by the wicked cities of the American hinterland, deep mines, and company stores; they recounted our pitifully few conquests and reflected our impoverished and isolated lives. The music boiled in our blood the week around; through the hot work of the grain harvest, in the fearful soul-searching of midweek prayer meetings, up and down endless rows as we picked cotton nobody had the money to take off our hands. In our unpainted rural farmhouse in Eastland County, Texas — where one generation had died, one grew to adulthood, and still another was born — that music from our old Zenith battery radio reaffirmed our troubles and refurbished our dreams."

Jimmie Rodgers was ahead of us in so many ways that we installed him as the first member of The Country Music Hall of Fame in Nashville. But this was a good twenty years after country kids like me were imitating his guitar strums and his blue yodels. Jimmie had died seven months after I was born, but his voice was still at the back of our daily lives, such a sad, pure naive voice even when it was singing cocky about the mamas Jimmie had had. It seemed like the little Mississippi Brakeman had gone from the church in the wildwood to the honky-tonks on the highway and had lost everything (even his precious obscurity) except his innocence. Even then, as a towhead in the ticks and sand, I liked Jimmie Rodgers best when he was singing alone with his guitar and not backed by some Hawaiian-sounding studio orchestra. "They oughta not try to make Jimmie sound fancy," we used to complain, but still, long after his death, we listened to his recordings on the radio. It never occurred to us to go to the expense of buying a phonograph and the records themselves. That was for rich folks.

Jimmie was No. 1. And then there was Roy Acuff, and, after Roy it had to be Ernest Tubb, if you were down in Texas: Tubb and Bob Wills.

The greatest group singers were the Carter Family from Maces Spring, Va. There was the daddy, Alvin Pleasant Carter, the mother, Sara, and A.P.'s sister-in-law, Maybelle Addington Carter. Maybelle was the best instrumentalist. She played autoharp, banjo and guitar and sang alto. A.P. could play the fiddle when he had to and sang bass. Sara could play a little on several instruments, but mostly she sang lead. A.P. wrote the songs, many of which came from oral traditions. They sang them through their noses in a fine, tight harmony that would slip through you like homemade ice cream. Their classic was "Wildwood Flower" because it combined the best of their singing and Maybelle's great guitar style, which was so original that the great Leadbelly and Woody Guthrie would imitate her licks. The Carter Family and Jimmie Rodgers dominated country radio. Long after the Carters stopped recording in 1941, we could hear them deep in Texas on the powerful Mexican border radio stations.

Our love of hillbilly music took full and twangy expression while we were at Corpus. Uncle Earl and Aunt Arbie chipped in to pay for music lessons. I took guitar and my brother Bobby was given the family heirloom — Grandpa Henry Porterfield's fiddle — to learn to scratch upon. Our teachers were Professor Gartland and wife, who lived in the world's tiniest trailerhouse near the carnival on North Beach. The professor was a tall, rangy dignity who in his years as a violinist had gained little but a big belly, a mane of yellowish-gray hair and a beautiful blonde wife twenty years his junior. He taught strings, she the horns and percussion. They couldn't have made much from their pupils, living as they were on the gaudy beach, and you knew that both had started out with something higher in mind. But they were as dedicated as they were versatile, and taught with a patience and a love that was so infectious that the professor decided to organize the best of his pupils into a band. The oldest members, other than the Gartlands (the professor led the band and played fiddle; Mrs. Gartland took turns on horns) were twenty-year-old yellow-haired twin beauties who blew very loud saxophones and libido. I thumped my four chords and sang in my high soprano most of the solos while Brother Bobby fiddled and sang harmony. We called ourselves the Corpus Christi Corncobbers and we played for USO dances all during the war. Corpus was a big naval base and the town jumped during those years. We had a set opener. The professor would appear under the lights before the band, elegant in black tie and tails, violin under his arm. He would announce that he was opening the show with Beethoven. He'd cradle the violin into his neck, bend his great head down, and launch into the noble and dramtic Kreutzer Sonata. The audience, being sailors and their girls, would murmur and fall into a stunned hush. This was not what they had expected. But just as you could feel their hearts fall, the professor would shift gear and slide in an adroit bar from Beethoven into that rollicking reel, "Turkey in the Straw." By the time he finished the room was his, every sailor in his hand. The curtain or the lights would go up, and our band would break forth behind the professor with our theme song, "San Antonio Rose," which we picked up from Bob Wills. Now, 40 years later, it is hard to imagine that The Corncobbers were any good or that those 20-year-old sailors were very selective, but with all those horns and percussions the professor obviously was trying to make us a novelty band that ranged from the corny to country and pop. At least, he kept us booked.

When we weren't playing dances, Bob and I entertained guests in our home. Daddy would huddle with us in a back bedroom, thump us on the head with his hard, heavy index finger, and send us forth in concert with the admonition, "Now I want you boys to put that music on the top shelf," meaning we had better do our best. Mother often sang hymns with us. She had a fetching alto which blended with Bobby's tenor and my lead. I was the least musical of the lot, which was why I had the straight part. Of course we sang through our noses, Carter Family style, and it was deeply satisfying to us, if not our listeners. Later, though we were Baptists who often went to the Methodist church, Bobby and I sang and played for services at a Holy Roller church in Woodsboro. I never did anything with my music after that, which is an indication of how limited my talent was, but it deepened my appreciation of the truly gifted, and, years later even as my musical taste broadened I never lost my ear for Jimmie Rodgers and the Carter Family. And in that Valhalla I put the old music professor of North Beach, as heroic a failure as they come in trailerhouses.

We all need heroes, models, someone to look up to. Some of us are more demanding of our heroes than others. Instant celebrities bore me. Most of my heroes are dead, and the ones that are still kicking are long in the tooth. I suppose that's because I like them a mite old-fashioned; I like them to hang in there over the long haul. I like them to be human, to be flawed, to be capable of injury and humiliation, to be able to endure obscurity like the rest of us before making a comeback. That was the way Jimmie Rodgers was. That is the way a contemporary singer like Mickey Gilley is.

Still, Ernest Tubb's pluck tops them all. The old troubadour from Crisp, Texas, turning 70 in 1984, is still on the road in his Silver Eagle touring bus, making more than 200 appearances a year and logging a hundred thousand miles a year across the Southland. In our trek across the honky-tonk states of Texas, we were always arriving before Ernest and his Texas Troubadours were to play or after they had packed up and gone. No honky-tonk was too small or out of the way for Ernest. He loves to reach his fans, yes, but part of the reason he maintains such a man-killing pace is that his records are not played and promoted the way they were in the golden days. If the record company and the radio stations and the jukebox vendors won't toot his old horn, Ernest will toot it himself until he drops dead on the road. He can't sing any better than you and me. But then, that's always been the case. To hear Ernest was to hear your uncle, the one that lost his farm to the bankers and lost his heart to a good-looking mama who treated him like dirt. It wasn't pretty singing, but Lord, it was real. Out of the old rock.

When someone asks me who my heroes outside country music are, I always imagine them making up the roster of some country town baseball team. I used to watch a lot of those cow pasture games on Sunday afternoons. Here's my fife and drum, five and dime American Dream Team: Walt Whitman would sing the national anthem to start things off. Grover Cleveland, that obstinate bull of a man, would be catcher. Abe Lincoln on first, Mark Twain on second, Harry Truman at shortstop and Carl Sandburg on third. In the outfield I'd have Sam Houston, Andrew Jackson and Franklin Delano Roosevelt, sluggers all. The designated hitter would be Teddy Roosevelt. What rascals, but, like Ruth, they had clout. Pitchers would be Tom Jefferson, Will Rogers, Robert Frost, William Faulkner and J. Frank Dobie. John Adams would be the pilot, George Washington the general manager and Uncle Sam the owner. Blackie Sherrod would be in the press box, Katharine Hepburn the gal reporter trying to get into the locker room, and, of course, Clarence Darrow would represent her in court. Since I'm the scout for my American Dream Team, I guess I can sign up John Henry Faulk as our number one reliever.

Well now, filling the same positions with an all-star lineup of country musicians might be fun. Let's see. I'd ask Woody Guthrie to sing the national anthem. I want to start things off in an authentic way with those closest to the folk, those, in John Greenway's phrase, "who rarely stray far from the Anglo-Saxon word-hoard." But wait, let's don't play any more games. I'll just talk straight and forget the baseball metaphor.

A couple of springs ago, NBC televised a tribute to Roy Acuff, noting that for 50 years he had been the king of country music. They had a telling way to open the show. A young Acuff, circa 1940, came on with his Smoky Mountain Boys playing and singing "The Great Speckle Bird."

Fade.

On came an old Roy Acuff, circa 1982, still backed by the Smoky Mountain Boys — all showing their age — to finish the song they started singing in 1936.

The way we warp time with film and tape is still a wonder, but that's not what struck me that March night. What hit me, and moved me, was the realization of how little Acuff and his musicians have changed over the years. I'm talking about their music, not their mugs. In this lickety-split age, it's reassuring to see something stay put for a while. Roy and his boys are sticks-in-the-mud, but it is native clay, the dearest old dough ever baked in the blue-eyed Appalachian sun.

The songs Acuff sings are wrought from mountain air and wilderness, but at a time when the locomotives and electricity of urban America were cutting into the Great Smoky, the Blue Ridge and the Cumberland mountains, uprooting a clan of nesters who were almost Elizabethan in their hold on attitudes and airs they had brought from the British Isles a hundred years before.

So there is a clash of cultures in Acuff's music that is richly American. If his fiddles and banjos dance a highland jig, his voice soars from a sweet yodel to the mournful imitation of a train whistle, and in his ballads is the lament of a people passing from one kind of life to another.

"Bird," the first song they recorded in 1936, and "Wabash Cannon Ball," waxed in that same historic session, have remained the two great songs with which Acuff is identified. Listen to "Great Speckle(d) Bird." Roy didn't write it; he picked it up from his people. It was made up by an old mountain preacher, and it is, in Bill Malone's words, "faintly metaphysical." It is taken from the Bible, Jeremiah 12:9, which says that "Mine heritage is unto me as a speckled bird, the birds round about are against her." And it is about backwoods Christians going through hell on earth as they await Heaven and Kingdom Come. Anyone over 40 who has ever sat in a congregation of white Southern fundamentalists, especially Pentecostals, has heard every verse of it. Acuff just made it popular beyond the hollows and gaps. In "Wabash Cannon Ball," the secular reality of a country and a people in transition overtakes us as an iron horse flashes past, rumbling and roaring, taking in its clacking bosom an old hobo hitchhiker, who dreams that he will be carried to the wonderful land of his fantasy.

The music Acuff makes is as pure a folk idiom as is left in Nashville. For all his success as a performer, composer, publisher and promoter of young talent, for all the wealth and renown that could corrupt, Acuff is still the mountain boy from Maynardsville, Tennessee. It is incredible that he has been able to keep himself thus, even as he approaches 82 years of age. Perhaps it is because his wife, Mildred, and his partner, Fred Rose, were the brains of their business and protected Roy from the mundanities and the compromises. But I doubt that.

The key is Acuff himself. "I've never had enough sense or talent to be anything other than myself," he says. Certainly, as the host and No. 1 star of the Grand Ole Opry, Roy has not shielded himself from the trends that keep flashing in spangles through country music. He just hasn't gone along himself, except as a friend and promoter of others and as a straight man to Minnie Pearl. I've never seen him wear a sequin, and I'd bet his fiddle isn't wired for sound. The old microphone will do, thank you. It doesn't matter that he can't sing like he used to. It is enough that he opens his mouth.

The two-hour tribute to Roy was, save for the homage and history, simply an elongated Opry moved to a prime-time week spot. It was good to hear some of Roy's old colleagues — Eddy Arnold (who can still sing), Hank Snow, Ernest Tubb, Kitty Wells, Bill Monroe, etc. And it was a bore to hear the slick country stars of today. The only youngsters on the show who deserved to stand by the king himself were Emmy Lou Harris and Charlie Daniels, and, of course, the son of another king, Hank Williams Jr.

Yeah, I have a bone to pick.

Barbara Mandrell sings that she was country when country wasn't cool, but you can't be sure by listening to her songs. I don't care how many awards she wins, she ain't country. She's Miss Slick, too homogenized with pop and the possibilities of the blandly commercial to impress the sensitive ear. Oh, Mandrell's perky cute and a little dynamo, but the music she makes is mediocre, even bad. What's the point of playing all those instruments if you play them poorly? Ask any journeyman musician. Her voice is a competent blend of the indistinctive. It is not immediately recognizable.

Of course, Mandrell is popular, perhaps the hottest female singer in that amorphous and profitable market which keeps crossing over between country and pop. Loretta Lynn is all but retired, and Dolly Parton is going off into so many directions, musical and otherwise, that she just goes through the motion of recording, tossing off hits that sound metallic and manufactured, empty of everything except a tired, technical savvy and a great voice. The same thing happened to Kenny Rogers years ago. Once, in his First Edition days, Rogers was an innovative musician. Now he is awful, awfully successful, and rich and ruined.

You can't say that Mandrell has sold out, because she didn't have anything to begin with. But Parton and Rogers have singular voices which made us listen, and now they've lost them in a trade with the devil. No wonder Rogers whispers. Ah, but what a tempting devil it is. Only the most original and stubborn artists can survive intact.

The difference between the great and the merely popular is that the great ones maintain their individuality in the face of the terrible demands of success. They become stars, yes, but they never lose the originality that launched them in the first place. They don't just coast on their talent and reputation. They continue to hone and refine their work, until one day it dawns on us that they have become masters, that in the forge of their invention, in the sweaty weld of pain and talent and craft, they have transcended cliché to touch the classic. We know them instantly, and they wear well. Everything they do is not great, but most everything, even their failures, bears the mark of a mature artist.

In country music, the old masters I'm talking about start with Jimmie Rodgers and come up to the present to George Jones. In between are troubadours like Hank Williams Sr., Merle Haggard, Willie Nelson and Waylon Jennings. They grow better with age, and their lives begin to take on the aura of legend. I'm looking for that to happen to young John Anderson. He's got it. Hank Williams Jr. is already on his way. Both ought to cure beautifully.

I have never been particularly interested in the personal lives of show biz celebrities. Someone suggested I read the piece on George Jones in *Texas Monthly*. This was back in July of 1982. They knew I liked old George's songs. Well, I can listen to George Jones every day on the stereo, but I wouldn't bother to read about him and his ups and downs. I get the idea listening to his laments, and it's art. In print, it would be trash.

Sometimes, most of the time, stardom is a psychological killer, especially in a land of parvenus. Racists look at sports figures like the Bob Hayeses and the Hollywood Hendersons and say that blacks can't stand up to the pressures and siren calls of celebrity. It's not blacks, bub, it's just poor folks in general who tend to run away with themselves when they turn from being a nobody to a somebody. Remember those fated rednecks Jimmie Rodgers and Hank Williams? And look at poor old George Jones. But then not every hick stumbles in the limelight. Some grow into prominence well. Charlie Pride isn't hurting.

Hank Williams Jr. says all his rowdy friends have settled down, but it isn't true. You see the wear and tear and grief on the old faces of the best singers. The ones who haven't killed themselves will, or come close to it. George Jones isn't going to straighten out. He just got indicted for cocaine while his daughter, Tamala Georgette, calls, "Daddy, oh Daddy, come home."

In J. Moffat and M. D. Henney's "Still Doin' Time," George sings:

> Has it been a year since the last time I've seen her?
> My God, I would swear it was 10.
> And the ocean of liquor I drank to forget her
> Is gonna kill me, but I'll drink till then.
> I been living in hell
> With a bar for a cell,
> Still payin' for my cheatin' crime.
> Oh, and I've got a long way to go.

> Still doin' time.
> Still doin' time
> In a honky-tonk prison,
> Still doin' time
> Where a man ain't forgiven.
> My poor heart is breakin',
> Oh, but there's no escapin'.
> Each morning I wake up and I find,
> Still doin' time.

George is up Whisky Creek, but Merle's trying to be good and so is Willie. Haven't heard much lately from Waylon on that score. It doesn't really matter. What matters is their music. It contains the best of them. The rest is slag, the leftover from too much burnout. High-octane art is inflammable and eventually consumes the artist. Hank Williams Jr. knows it, even as he lights up. As he says, it's a family tradition.

CHAPTER 5

Our Red Necks

"After all, what is position if one can't do a day's work, tame a woman, and whip a little ass if he needs to?"
— *James Ward Lee*
in *"Bury My Heart At Wounded Neck"*

It seems to me that I spent most of my boyhood in the rear seat of a black Terraplane Hudson staring at the back of my father's wrinkled red neck as we droned across the Texas prairie from one oil patch to the next. I can still hear the engine and the whine of that transmission. It is like a mother's heartbeat. I can smell the faded felt of the seats. The telephone poles and their crossbars flash past like crucifixes. We could get so far out from nowhere that we left the poles behind, and there would be nothing but the ribbon of road amid all that time and space.

On those endless odysseys, the destinations proved to be mirages — dreamy reststops half-remembered — for we never got to where we were going and have yet to complete the journey. We may have gotten to the rig where Daddy was to work but that's another thing entirely. Even the work itself was transitory, a means to an end. If the work seemed more real — it was clangingly loud in its effort and brutally demanding of a roughneck's body — it was only because a screaming drilling rig made a greater assault on the senses than the nagging dream that drove us across the Southwest. Still the end we sought was more insistent than the Protestant work ethic that towed us from job to job. It was just harder to define. Each of us made stabs at it, but with little success. We had our notions about what we were about. Mother decided that Daddy's get-up-and-go was meant to drive her crazy. Poor woman. She went to her grave fully expecting that the Heavenly journey was an eternal circling about on the dusty roads of Limbo, a higher version of the Porterfield-Joads on their way to God knows where. I think it is telling that my father still lives on wheels. It is as if at any moment, even at the stiff and sore age of 81, he must pack up and hit the road in one last attempt to finish what he began when he left an Oklahoma farm.

And yet there were compensations on the road. We were not in a hurry in those days. Forty miles an hour was it. It didn't have to be. The speedometer on that old Terraplane had 120 miles an hour on it. Pa liked to poke along. We went from A to B to C and so on, and if we never got to Z before dark, that was fine. We could be waylaid by anything of interest we thought we would see even if it meant getting off the pavement and heading off into the flats.

I remember one hot-as-tarnation August we were coming down off the Llano Estacado along the Texas-New Mexico border. We were weary. The Staked Plain is the longest and flattest table of land in the world, and Mother was counting the miles to Lubbock, where she could collapse in a tourist cabin. But Pa drove right past Lubbock just as slick as you please. Ma was fit to be tied. What in heaven's name did he think he was up to?

"I'm headin' for Seminole," he said lightly. "There's an old Indian chief out there who'll tell your fortune for a shot of whiskey. One time he told me I would fall from a rig and nearly kill myself and, sure enough, I did. He told me I'd marry a pretty little curly-haired gal from Indiana and sure enough, I did."

Mother was not about to be placated by such as that. She made Daddy stop the car so she could get in the back seat with us kids. She didn't speak to him for a hundred miles.

When we got to Seminole, which was as sad as a huddle of shacks on a desolate and windy plain, Daddy found the old Indian sitting on his porch.

"Chief Wa Who," he said, "long time no see. Me Tice Porterfield. You remember?"

The Indian looked at him blankly.

"Me bring whiskey," Daddy said, offering the old man a snort of something raw he had been carrying under the car seat. "You tell fortune."

The Indian took a good shot.

We kids gathered around. Mother remained in the car, her eyes almost crossed with disapproval. Daddy gave us a wink. He offered a palm to the Indian. "What do you see, Wa Who?"

"Hard to say," the old man said. "More whiskey."

It went on like that until the half pint was almost empty.

Pa was getting impatient. "Come on, Chief Wa Who," he said. "Read my palm. We've got to get to Odessa before dark."

The old man again took Daddy's hand and studied it.

"Me see angry woman," he said.

"What else?"

"That all."

"That's all?" Daddy roared. "You can't tell me nothin' more'n that?"

"Angry woman," the old man said. "That all. That enough."

We laughed at Daddy's expense all the way to Odessa, and Mother led the mocking chorus. Pa never said a word. His neck just got redder.

For all we knew, that old Indian might have been mayor of the town and a graduate of Harvard University with a Ph.D. in pulling tourists' legs. Mother saved her biggest dig at Daddy for bedtime, when she climbed into bed with us kids and left him to sleep alone. That was one of her ways of getting back at him, and it worked. The next day he would be sweet as pie.

There were countless times, in our trips across the land, that I concentrated on the faces and physical peculiarities of my kin in the car. But it is the neck of my father that I remember the most. I might have remembered Mother's neck, but I don't think I ever saw it because her hair was in the way. The term redneck is not used loosely here. There was not a pale male neck in that car, not in that country. Man or boy, we had played and labored long in the Texas sun. It made its mark on us. I still remember the variety of wrinkles and hues the sun wrought on our vulnerable scruffs. My brother, younger by 10 months, wore a tender, pink expression on the back of his skinny neck. My father's was deeper and tanner, more manly. You could read a man's character in his neck. Daddy's neck said that he was hardworking and capable, and, frankly, a little thickheaded. A good man, in balance, if always stubborn and sometimes cruel. Grandpa's neck was a curious combination of my father's and my brother's, and freckled. There was something in his neck, a delicacy, that told you that he was more than a country man. He never totally revealed himself to us. There was a mystery about him, a hint of it in his neck. But the neck I most want to tell you about was that of Glen Thomas, a stringbean of a boy I knew in one of the towns. Glen had a hard, reddest-of-the-red neck, a mean, bony, stubborn neck that matched his manner. It was a neck that I came to hate as I have no other neck.

Glen and I used to wrestle a lot, "rassle" we called it, and I, being shorter and quicker, could usually get him down in the dust with an armlock. My intention was to make him say "uncle." Yet I remember, still with a strong sense of frustration and failure, that he never said it with me around his neck. I could tighten my hold like a vise, until I was red in the face and gritting my teeth and he was choking and as bug-eyed as Carrie Cude — who was afflicted with glaucoma — and we could flounder around in the schoolyard dirt that way for the whole morning recess and still Glen wouldn't give up, wouldn't say that one silly word of submission. I started each match with new resolve, having failed the previous times, and I still feel the acute regret that would ooze into my mind, indeed into the depth of my heart, when my strength would finally, inexorably begin to ebb, until out of my numb arms would squirm Glen Thomas and his unconquerable neck. I became easy prey. My best and most sustained offense he had withstood. My arms were weary as rags, I had no heart, no fight left. He would lunge upon me, pin me to the ground with his left armlock and proceed to choke me until I had fainted. Neither of us had said "uncle," but clearly he had won. A crowd always gathered for the match and most of the spectators, especially the girls, would pull for me. Vanquished, shamed, I would stagger to my feet and limp to the shade and solitude of the fountain, where I would bathe my pride and hide my tears in splashes of water.

But even in winning, Glen Thomas never got his due. He was all the wrong things. He was skinny as hunger, more cross-eyed than Aunt Sarah, and left-handed. He was hard and mean, a brute who was liked only by other brutes. Yet he always won in the end. He had that staying power peculiar to unwanted things. He was a redneck.

I think of those retarded but tough cedars that grow out of the rock in the hill country. Or of Raff Ardmore's mongrel tearing up better-bred and cared-for dogs. I could not match this survival of the unfit, the unwashed and unwanted, with the admonition, especially Granny's, to be like Jesus. I could see Jesus winning souls and turning his cheek while losing the world to a tribe in common with Glen Thomas.

Everybody has to have someone to look down on.

I say Glen was a redneck. At the time we wouldn't have called him that. He was, in Mother's words, white trash. There was a difference. Way before I was born, redneck was not a term of derision, at least it wasn't to country folk. It was what set us apart from townspeople. We toiled in the sun growing things and would not have lived in town for anything. Daddy always had a basic distrust of men who wore white collars and suits every day and who had soft, white, womanly hands and shiny shoes. He had known Woody Guthrie in the Oklahoma Dust Bowl days and they had always said, "Some rob you with a gun, some with a fountain pen." Somehow, the gun seemed more direct, and therefore more honest. People from town were dudes and jellybeans if they lived on the right side of the tracks and white trash if they lived on the wrong side. Dudes cheated you with sleight-of-hand, and white trash were such shiftless chiselers that they would go on the public dole before they would turn their hand to a lick of work. But I'm getting ahead of myself. I want to go back and try to trace the evolution of the redneck as I see it from my family's vantage point.

You see, within the context of today's meaning of redneck, we did not start out rednecks. I told a friend this the other day, and he smiled and shot back, "Okay, you were blond gypsies."

Well, that comes close, but not quite. I have had gypsies read my fortune. I have had gypsies sell me their handiwork. I have had gypsies tell me the strangest and most beautiful stories, tales that left me jealous and wishing I was a gypsy, too. I have danced with gypsies at their wedding feasts and I have wailed with gypsies at the death of their kings. There is even the touch of the gypsy in that dark, intuitive little woman I knew as my mother. The road knows we lived like gypsies, following the rigs the way we did. But for all our wandering, for all our love of fiddles and songs and stories and the adventure ahead, we were not gypsies, at least not of the Romany kind so legendary and mysterious. We had come from another part of the world. If we were restless and rollicking and full of folkways it was because the Celts in our past were still very much present.

Just about the time I think I've outlived them, lived them down and am my my own man, they swarm back to slap me in place. My father's side of the family were the Scotch and Irish who filled up the American South, and my mother's side were much the same, save for some Black Dutch in the woodpile.

The Anglo-Celts who began streaming into the Southwest in the 1820s were entirely different invaders from the Spanish and the French who had preceded them. Once Scot borderers, they had mixed blood with the Dane and the Gael and the Saxon of the Teutonic South, and had evolved into a tough and stubborn people. Dour is the way historian T. R. Fehrenbach describes them, conditioned to war. They fought the English for generations, although they themselves had been speaking English for hundreds of years.

John Knox gave them a sense of being God's Chosen People — this they shared with the Spanish, along with an arrogant racism — and they saw themselves as being on a beeline of divine purpose from Genesis to Judgment Day. Flinty, restless, they had spun out of the British Isles and had swarmed by the boatland into the New World. Three generations on the American frontier had sharpened their wit and skill and endurance.

If the Spanish and French in the New World had been swashbucklers and cavaliers, the Anglo-Celts were root-hog-or-die hunters and sodbusters. The Spanish and French had come to look for silver and gold, and, although they claimed the land of the Indians for their kings, individually the explorers and soldiers were not bent on staying here. They did not colonize, but came, conquered, incorporated, and left the celibate priests to try to pacify and convert the natives. The Anglo-Celts had something more permanent in mind. Dissidents, diehards, they were refugees on the prowl for a place in the New World sun, a spot where no one would bother them. Walt Whitman sang that they were

>Those that look carelessly in the faces
>   of Presidents and governors, as if to say,
>"Who are you?"
>Those of earth-born passion, simple,
>   never constrained, never obedient,
>Those of inland America.

They came not seeking quick gold or silver, but to find a new beginning and a new home. Cortes and La Salle had come at the behest of their governments. The Anglo-Celts came at the suggestion of no one but their own. They were tall, rawboned (well, some of us weren't), and they bred like rabbits. My father was one of nine sons and two daughters. They filled the plains with blue-eyed, towheaded children. Once Presbyterians, they were now Baptists and Methodists with a decided Calvinist cast. They came bearing Bibles and long rifles and they ran over everything in their path. In his monumental work, *Lone Star: A History of Texas and the Texans,* Fehrenbach describes them this way:

"They were not going to retreat. They were poised to attack, a tough, hungry, numerous, riotous, and yet curiously disciplined horde. They were moving out of cultural time, to devour limitless space. They had no banners, armies, or grand leaders, no real rationale for conquest. They had their long rifles and sad songs, their fiddlers and graybeards, their chopping axes and their essentially gloomy grasp of life."

* * *

They sound like my paternal grandfather.

In a book called *Growing Up in Texas,* I describe my father's family, beginning with my grandfather, Henry Mack: "He was a stern and patriarchal man ... He thrashed and worked them (his children) when they were rambunctious, and at dusk, when they were milk-sopped and subdued, he played them ballads and jigs on his fiddle. This seems a wonderful life to me, a Populist reverie dreamed up by Vachel Lindsay and Edgar Lee Masters. But to my father and his brothers, it was a hard row to hoe, especially with the lights and lure of the oil field boomtowns at their back door. The fields at Nowata, Bartlesville, Glenn Pool, Cushing and Healdton had been discovered, and Oklahoma was suddenly the world's bonanza for black gold. Cotton patches had become a forest of derricks, and quiet communities like Tulsa and Ardmore were transformed into brawling meccas for roughnecks with money to burn. How was a man to keep his sons down on the farm?

"Henry Porterfield could not.

"By 1920, eight years before Grandpa's death, the Industrial Revolution had struck the community of Old Hewitt a blow from which it would never recover. All the Porterfield boys, save one, had left to seek their fortunes following the drilling rigs. At 14, my father hired out in the nearby oil fields as a mule skinner. By the time he was 17, he had left home and was roughnecking, and within seven years he would be a driller, the man who hired and fired the roughnecks and ran the rig on shifts. It was dangerous, clamorous work that left you muddy and greasy and worn out after a 12-hour tour, but it was good hourly pay, seven days a week as long as it took to drill the well. The drawback was that the work was never constant. When you finished one job, you were either laid off or sent to another location. Often these locations were far apart, sometimes in another state, and there was an interval of weeks, or months, before the rig could be dismantled and moved and set up again. This meant lost time to the driller and his crew, and there were no such things as paid vacations and fringe benefits. You moved your family and your possessions at your own expense, and every idle hour was money out of your pocket."

Something was happening to my father that had not happened to his father. Henry Mack had stayed put on the Oklahoma farm, and between his plowing and praying and fiddling he had become a man of some substance. He owned land and mules and horses, house, barn and tools. He hired hands and gave orders as a deacon even told the preacher what to do. Henry was a figure to be reckoned with around Old Hewitt. Even the bankers in town got up to shake his hand. But now his son was out in the oil patch, working for wages, taking orders instead of giving them. It's true the pay was good in working men's estimation, but it wasn't steady, what with the stopping and starting and moving about. Tice Covey Porterfield had become an oily son of machinery and motion. He rented instead of owned. He rested on wheels instead of roots. He was often a stranger in a place and could offer no references except his own word and the character in his face, which was considerable but which counted for less and less in a society where numbers and accounts were beginning to be more important and trustworthy than a fellow's eye and handshake. In that new gauge of a man's worth, oilfield gypsies came up short.

It was even happening to the Henry Macks on the farms, and had been since the Yankees started coming down after the Civil War. In Texas in 1860, most white farmers were freeholders. A generation later, most were tenants. Bankers and merchants were audacious, hiking interest rates as high as 60 percent. By 1891 there were three million folks in the state and most were farmers and ranchers who didn't own clear title to the land they worked and had a hard time making a go of it. You either raised cattle or you grew cotton, and there wasn't much of a market for either. Down on the farm the feeling was that middlemen from the East had sucked us dry and Yankee creditors were licking the bones. Bankers were perceived as Shylocks, railroad magnates as landhogs, and corporations as monopolistic octopuses. It was a bitter time but a passionate time. The Texas agrarian movement was in full sway, and the hope of the Populists lay in the new governor, big fat Jim Hogg, who declared war on big business and the "soulless corporation." Now we know that it was just so much spitting in the wind, that even with William Jennings Bryan the family farmer was a flickering match in the wind of the new industrial age.

One of the ways to understand a society in flux is to look at its crime rate and the character of its criminals. So the other day when my eyes fell upon a list of fugitives from justice in Texas in 1891, compiled at the time by the adjutant general's office, I couldn't help but read it with fascination. Save for some strange psychopathic personalities here and there — people who would have been criminals in any age — most of the outlaws resembled the everyday folk I grew up with. Their crimes were improbities against property or the sexual and moral codes of the day. Not only was there a war between the haves and have-nots, there was a line being drawn between the poor themselves. In a culture fracturing and re-forming, even close families were being rent between their members who were God-fearing and fundamental in their faith and social mores and their members who were breaking away from the old taboos and starting to shake a leg along the outskirts of city life. It became another difference between my paternal grandfather and my father. Henry Mack may have played his pure mountain fiddle, but he stayed sober and pious and close to home and the straight and narrow. Son Tice kicked up his heels and drank his whiskey in the boom towns and hardly ever went to church with the wife and kids. Still, he was a family man. He always took us dancing with him. Mother's father, Daddy Harrell, had done the same thing, which was why Henry Mack never approved of him socially while acknowledging that he was a fine farrier.

Depressions and hard times have come and gone, along with Prohibition and Ma and Pa Ferguson. The family farm has become the syndicate, the small town square a huddle of ghosts, while the cities burgeon like Sodom and Gomorrah. Poor have become rich, and rich have become poor, and between them is a giant middle class. We have gone to the moon and can make babies in a test tube. But you still can't get a drink in half of Texas because of this old division between the hymn-singers and the honky-tonkers. My problem, as usual, is that I love both camps. Each is an understandable escape from the powers that be who still lord over us at work and in the marketplace.

Yes, I have a bone to pick with them that sit on our necks. Jim Hogg may have been a phony poor man and Ma and Pa may have been crooked, but I'm still a Populist, still an underdog, still a redneck even if I like blacks and browns and eggheads like Adlai Stevenson and Eugene McCarthy. Every redneck didn't stand in the schoolhouse door with George Wallace. No sir. You don't have to march with the Klan and go cross-eyed over the evils of race-mixing and evolution to stay in the fraternity. Don't have to look for communists under the bed. Don't have to love guns and trucks and talk on the CB.

All you have to do to be a redneck is to have been born in the blood and testament and to realize it and acknowledge it even if you hate it. You have to burn in the sun, still show a freckle. You have to know and love the hymns even if you've strayed. You can fight the old man till the day you die, but you must love mother even if she's a nasty old toad. You must have hayseed taste, such as an irresistible urge to whitewash the trunks of trees. You must eat barbecue and chicken-fried steak, drink beer and bourbon, boss your lady (or try to), breed more kids and keep more dogs and cars than you can afford, hate the city and yearn for the country. But your biggest hate has to be against authority, anyone or any establishment or state that won't let you be. This means, of course, that you can't be one of the big boys, one of the yes and no men. If a redneck graduates to that level, he's no longer a redneck but a good old boy. As Bob Dylan sings, "You've got to serve somebody." You can't like it. You can't lick. You'd rather die. What you do is keep a chip on your shoulder and a bitch on your lips. The catch is that to remain a real redneck means you are suspended between anger and impotence. You can do little about them that sit on your neck. You can't get together and compromise enough to be an effective political force. And personally you know you'll never get ahead at work, you'll always be hard up for money.

Talk of recession or depression doesn't bother you. All it means is business as usual. Your whole life has been a recession. It is all you know, and you're not sure you want somebody coming along and screwing things up by making them better.

Like an Appalachian dunce at the foot of the class, full of hookworms and hominy, I squinch up my potato-bead eyes, furrow the brow of my turnip face, and try to imagine the opposite of depression. I come up with economic stability, even prosperity. The thought of such a thing is petrifying. No Porterfield worthy of the name (and there have been dang few backsliders) ever served up such as that to wife and kids. Them that did were a breed apart. That would be like putting raisins in the haggis or getting a new suit for graduation. I mean, it just wasn't done. We told ourselves that ostentation was not in our vocabulary, except when we leveled the accusation of it at others.

I'll never forget the look on Mother's face when one of our neighbors, Lodemia Nowlan, showed up for her baptism wearing a new dress from Curlee's Department Store in Victoria. Now Lodemia was the local beautician — no more, no less than the rest of us. "Well, look at Miss Swell," Ma had said, and she held it against her for some time. I thought she was being a mite severe, couldn't help but smile years later when, on her deathbed, Ma sent Pa out to buy a new suit for her funeral.

Weeks before she died, Mother was still sending me money as she always had, $5 or $10 a month, the bill hidden in the fold of a page torn from a Chief writing tablet. And here I was, a man well into his 40's with grown kids of his own who were still on his tit. What did I do with the money? I welcomed it and spent it gladly, just as my children do with what geetus I give them.

You see, it was okay to pass greenbacks back and forth with family and friends. This way, the money went around to where it was most needed. No one got piggy about it, pride being what it is, and the money circulated from hand to hand within the circle of love and blood. Well, it wasn't always love, you understand, families being what they are. Still, we were thick. No one was above need. It could happen to any of us from time to time, though we all (most of us, that is) strived. The best thing about that system was that there were no middlemen, no money changers to take their bite out of it. The charging of interest never occurred to us and we held no one to a strict accounting. It would even out anyway, by-and-by. We were all in the same boat.

This is not to say that we thought of ourselves as poor. Being poor was not being destitute, so down and out in health and spirit and whatever that you couldn't work and get along. People who got that way out of circumstance were to be pitied. People who got that way out of inheritance and made a habit of it were white trash. They were almost as guilty in our eyes as those who are born rich. A man on alms, whether the public's or his Pa's, was not a full man. Still and all, we couldn't help feeling compassion for people who have a hard time of it. Like Jesus Christ and Abe Lincoln, we had a natural affinity for underdogs and reckoned that it's usually more than their own shiftlessness that keeps them down. Is it any wonder that they are contemptuous of the law when they've never known the high side of it but know well the low? Is it any wonder that sometimes they rob and steal for pennies when they see the rich murder their own and get off free, when corporations rob with a fountain pen and politicians, particularly in Texas, get away with taking bribes? When people at the top cheat, it makes it hard for those on the bottom to keep it clean in their struggle to survive.

Daddy always thought of himself as a workingman. Even between jobs, when times were tight and we had to eat poor-man pie (stale bread baked in a blend of cream — from the cow — and sugar and cinnamon), there was never any kowtowing to self-pity. "This is nothing," the old man would say, and then bore us with his dissertation on The Great Depression.

It's funny how blissful ignorance is, how sweetly life makes things relevant. Just this past weekend, my father reared back in his trailerhouse and allowed, with satisfaction, that he had always made good money. "I drew top dollar," he said. And it was true, according to his lights.

I looked at him and realized that I've never really broken away from him and the rest of the family. How I earn my keep is a little different, but it's still drawing wages. I still live from payday to payday as we always did. I wouldn't know what to do with extra money lying around. I would waste away into fruitless indolence, end up as soft and sated as a Mongolian satyr I read about once. It's just as well. Indulge me this. Let me make virtue out of grief as you would any philosopher.

Now my brother, he feels differently. He is always going to make a wad of money one of these days. He is a salesman. They always think that way, and that attitude, as you would imagine, puts him in conflict with his workingman inheritance. A workingman works like a drudge for a living and only dreams of coming into money. You might hit oil on the old family farm. Something like that. You fancy it, but you don't count on it. Being rich is not one of life's constants. It is exotic, a far country, as mythical as Atlantis, and I don't expect my brother will ever get there.

He is, after all, a Porterfield, true to the blood in spite of himself.

Here I am waxing philosophical, but if you become a philosopher about being in such a state, you're screwed too, because that's as anathema to redneck culture as having money. In other words, you can't have any cents or sense. The only way out is through Jesus or Bacchus. Hank Williams Jr. suggests another. Grab your woman and towheads and head for the woods. Listen to his ditty:

> The interest is up
> And the stockmarket's down,
> And you only get mugged
> If you go downtown.

I live back in the woods, you see,
My woman and the kids and the dogs and me.
I got a shotgun, a rifle and a four-wheel drive,
And a country boy can survive.
Country folks can survive.

Because you can't starve us out and you can't make us run,
Cause we're them old boys raised on shotgun.
We say grace and we say ma'am
If you ain't into that, we don't give a damn.
And a country boy can survive,
Country folks can survive.

"A Country Boy Can Survive"
by Hank Williams, Jr.

CHAPTER 6

Our Womenfolk

There used to be but five kinds in Redneckville.

Mother

M is for the million things she gave me.
O means only that she's growing old.
T is for the tears were shed to save me.
H is for her heart of purest gold.
E is for her eyes with love-light shining.
R means right, and right she'll always be.

Put them all together,
They spell MOTHER,
A word that means the world,
To me.

"M-O-T-H-E-R"
by Howard Johnson and Theodore Morse

Sister

My mother was a lady
   like yours, you would allow.
And you may have a sister
   who needs protection now.
I've come to this great city
   to find my brother dear.
You wouldn't dare insult me, sir
   if Brother Jack were here.

"Mother Was a Lady"
by Edward B. Marks and Joseph W. Stern

The Sweetheart/Wife

Could I have this dance
For the rest of my life?
Would you be my partner
Every night?

"Could I Have This Dance"
by Wyland Holyfield and Bob House

Honky-Tonk Angels

I didn't know God made honky-tonk angels,
I might have known you'd never make a wife.
You gave up the only one who ever loved you,
And went back to the wild side of life.

"The Wild Side of Life"
by W. Warren and A. A. Carter

The Dream Woman

A redneck girl likes to cruise in daddy's pickup truck,
And a redneck girl plays her heart when she's down
    on her luck.

Livin' for Friday afternoon,
She's gonna show one old boy that weekend moon.

And I pray that someday I will find me a redneck girl.

A redneck girl likes to stay out all night long,
She makes sweet rock 'n roll while she listens to the
    country songs.

She's waitin' for that moment of surrender,
Her hands are calloused but her heart is tender.

Oh, gimme a, gimme a, gimme a redneck girl,
Gimme a, gimme a, gimme a redneck girl . . .

"Redneck Girl"
by The Bellamy Brothers

At least in rinky-tink, rinky-dink song there were but five states of womankind. The character of each type was cast and set, and there were no crossovers without a price. A woman was one or the other and there were no in-betweens. Of course, a woman could grow from being a sister to being someone's sweetheart/wife and mother. Or Sis and even the wife could fall from grace and become a honky-tonk angel, but even then it wasn't her fault. As Kitty Wells reminded us in J.D. Miller's song.

> It wasn't God who made honky-tonk angels,
> As you said in the words of your song;
> Too many times married men think they're still
>   single
> That has caused many a good girl to go wrong.
>
> *"It Wasn't God Who Made*
> *Honky-Tonk Angels"*
> *by J.D. Miller*

We were male chauvinists of the first water, and so, it seemed, were our womenfolk. At least they went along with it for years, seeming to allow us, in fact and in song, to mold their characters and define their roles. What idealizations they were on the one hand, and what profanities on the other. It's silly to suppose these women conjured up by their menfolk had anything to do with woman as reality. We were so sentimental about mom that she became sickeningly sweet. For a while sister suffered the same diabetes.

Who among us, we ex-bucolics over forty, who among us does not remember The Lodge Hall? That temple of male myth. Yours might have paid for itself by being a store, downstairs, selling soda pop and crackers, high octane and feed. The one I remember was content to remain locked and latently mysterious until Thursday nights when my father and his fraternal buddies filled it with even greater mystery, donning robes and lighting candles and crosses and chanting rites so secret that womenfolk and children could never know their meaning. These meetings, heady with blood oaths and omen, yet common as Thursday nights, became no less fantastic when I was inducted, at sixteen, as a member of the Demolay, a sort of junior Masonry. I recall being blindfolded and hooded and herded along with dozens of boys my age. We were placed in a processional and marched around the lodge until we arrived at an altar. Our hoods and blindfolds were removed, and we were made to bend and kiss an open Bible, grasp a thorny white rose, and swear upon all that was sacred that we would never molest or in any way defile or bring affront to a fellow Mason's wife, sister or daughter. I took it to mean that everyone else's was fair game.

Still, the little wife was too close for the kind of sugary comfort we felt toward mom and sis. A boy lived with his mother and sister, left them behind in a glow when he became a man and moved in with his new wife. Once the honeymoon was over, we stepped back and sobered up about the girl of our dreams. We stopped calling her sweetheart and sugar and honey and began calling her the wife and the old woman. I knew one husband who referred to his as the war department. In such daily proximity, we men had a chance to get to know our women as women instead of as figments of our imaginations, but we couldn't stand the revelation. Out of habit, we paid lip service to the marriage and the wife, but took our passions and dreams elsewhere. The beer joints and honky-tonks were the logical places to go. They were hidden on the edge of town. They were packed, day and night, with cigareetes and whuskey and wild, wild, women, the kind we thought were safe because they were just out looking for a good time, too, that's all. Oh, woe were we. They drove us crazy, they drove us insane.

> Once I was happy and had a good wife,
> I met with a gal, and we went
>   on a spree.
> She taught me to smoke
>   and drink whuskey.
> "Cigareetes, Whuskey and Wild, Wild Women"
>   by Tim Spencer

Remember Hank Williams singing, "Hey Good Lookin' "?

> I got a hotrod Ford and a two dollar bill,
> And I know a spot right over the hill.
> There's soda pop and the dancin's free,
> So if you wanna have fun come along with me.

Or Lefty Frizzell teaming with Jim Beck on "If You've Got the Money (I've Got the Time)"?

> If you've got the money, honey,
> I've got the time
> We'll go honky-tonkin' and we'll have a time.
> We'll make all the night spots,
>   dance, romance and dine . . .
> Bring along your Cadillac,
>   leave my old wreck behind . . .

Ah, but see, even in the early 1950's with Hank and Lefty, the honky-tonk woman was changing, coming into money and status enough to drive a Cadillac and even be taken out to eat on a date. What was happening in Middle America was taking place down here, too. Women were freeing themselves from the old restrictions of husband and home and children. They were crossing over and going back and forth so much between the old ways and new ones that no man with a lick of sense was going to call their bluff. It was too much trouble. Women were going, as my old man put it, "ever which way." It got to where none of the old characterizations applied. Women were no longer virginal white or scarlet red, good or bad. Even a nice girl like Barbara Mandrell could complain on the airways about sleeping single in a double bed. Even the Total Woman who wanted to go back to kitchen and kinder was politically pushy. The honky-tonks turned half-way respectable, at least many of them, and they became as crowded with mothers and sisters and wives, some legit and some on the sly, as the old country dance halls had been. Sanger D. Shafer said it all in a song he wrote for John Anderson:

> Angels and devils share the same tables,
> And that's not so wrong if you get it done right.
> Halos and horns lock up on the dance floor
> On a honky-tonk Saturday night.
>
> It's a honky-tonk Saturday night.
> It's not who is who
> It's who will or who might.
> With luck she'll turn on
>   before they turn out the lights
> On a honky-tonk Saturday night.

Floyd Berry and his wife, Ivy Dale, are regulars at Debonair Danceland in Dallas, one of the fine old stomping grounds for just folks, and while Floyd is happy that Ivy Dale has been sprung, so to speak — the kids are grown and she's retired from the laundry — he's also a mite concerned that she'll lose her cooking touch, especially with pie crusts and such. "She's going more and more to frozen foods and the microwave," he complained the other night while Ivy Dale was in the powder room.

"What does is matter?" I said, and launched into a description of the horrors of redneck mother cooking. I argued that we men had lost nothing in the transition from kitchen to dance floor, in fact had gained in the reclamation of our lost old loves who'd been waiting home for us all these years, just dying for us to take them out again.

To the Porterfields, food was fuel, a lump in the belly to ease a hunger pain and not something to savor. We hurried through meals, chomping and slurping, taking time to talk and be civil only at the Sunday dinners when the preacher was present. It is small wonder we did not linger over the essence of a particular vegetable or meat, because our women were as primitive in the preparing of a meal as the men were in disposing of it. There was not a good cook in the family. Texas women have always overcooked the best meats in the world, but Granny went one worse and fried her meat to damned near a cinder. Mother was not much more inventive. Neither had heard of broiling or boiling or baking a steer or pig or chicken. About the only meats they could not ruin were cured meats from the smokehouse. You would think the flavor of garden fresh vegetables would be retained on any country table, but not on the Porterfields'. Granny took Brother Reid's salt sermon to heart and sodium chlorided the bounty from the garden until I thought we would turn into Lot's wife. The old witch boiled vegetables in briny cauldrons until such a simple, evident thing as a stringbean was a mystery to the eye or the tongue.

Floyd stopped me in the middle of my harangue and said, "Look, that may have been your experience, and I'm sure it's shared by a good many others. But the fact of the matter is, Billy Porterfield, that Ivy Dale is the greatest pastry cook there is. No question in my mind about it."

"Which would you rather share with her?" I asked. "Her pie or her dancing?"

He leveled his gaze upon me and said, "Her pie. Hands down. But if you tell her I said that, I'll deny it, and when I get the chance I'll kill you."

So it's a mixed bag for us men.

I have no more saccharin illusions about my mother, not after all those years and having watched her fight a losing battle with cancer. We were able to say things to one another we had not before. Some terribly tender. Some the opposite.

One day, down at the trailer court in Seguin, Ma was admiring the glamor and get-up-and-go of the local Mary Kay cosmetic lady.

"Well," I said, "I'm sure all that's true, but don't you find that combination of piety, profit, pink Cadillac and mink a bit tacky?"

Ma looked at me hard. "Not any more than those old blue jeans and that cowboy hat you wear when you speak to the Unitarians for a measly fifty bucks."

After that, when I went home I tried to dress better and show a little more respect.

And that's what I did later back in Dallas when I went to the Mary Kay seminar at the convention center. And it worked. I looked past the Dolly Parton panache and found Glen Campbell's everyday housewife humming happily on her way to the bank. A woman of independent means is indeed a liberated woman, whether she is a Schlafly or a Steinem. The old gal behind it all, Mary Kay Ash, has to be something of a genius, a female cross between H. L. Hunt and Billy Graham with of course some snake oil and pied piping thrown in.

I wish now Mary Kay had come along a generation earlier to peddle her way around the poor white South. She might have made a difference in the lives of the women in our family. Gloria Steinem and Betty Friedan would have been too much too soon, absolutely wrong for our women. But Mary Kay, I think, might have been just right. Being poor, they would have perked up at a chance to make a little pocket money. And being feminine in the traditional sense, they would have liked the idea of staging beauty demonstrations in the homes of the neighbor ladies. In this way the husbands would not have been threatened.

Of all the women in our family, Cousin Crystal Ball would have been the best at this kind of thing. That is why I wished she could have been with me at the Mary Kay awards night. In my imagination I made her a brilliant blue lady of sales, called from the crowd to be crowned a unit queen, draped in mink and adored by all upon a white-trash-heaven stage.

My background qualifies me to use that expression. I use it with many-spangled irony, in much the same way that the "Magic of Mary Kay" set was designed. It was stunning, the most splendid thing this side of the Pearly Gates. It took me back to my childhood and my wildest dreams of what it would be like to die and go to heaven. Cousin Crystal Ball would have agreed.

You see, her life in particular was such a hillbilly hell that the only thing she could dream of as its exact opposite was a hillbilly heaven. Her husband Burl was a drunk and a ne'er-do-well and it was fitting, in a terrible kind of way, that he ended up tending the county dump. It was where he belonged, we used to say. The trouble was that his wife and kids had to share it with him. They lived in a shack behind the moldering mounds and everything they had in the house was a cast-off recovered from the dump. But Crystal Ball was a fine woman, a lady in spite of it all. My most vivid memory of her was the day in the dump when she put down her rake for a moment, not to rest, but to draw from her pocket a compact. She looked at herself in the mirror and rouged her cheeks and painted her pretty mouth with lipstick. Then she picked up the rake and went back to work spreading refuse.

Crystal Ball had a way of turning trash into treasure. At least she found utility in things that others would not bother with. But she also saw intrinsic value in what the rest of us considered junk. Take her plastic Clorox bottles. She would fish the white ones from the dump and cut and shape them into vases and flower pots, which she sold from a stand beside the shack. She put up a sign which read: "Imitation Marble Vases. 50¢ to $1." People bought them. But only, I imagine, after Crystal Ball showed them how to look at the vases. It was all in how you looked at them. "I don't see it," I told her one day. "They look like plastic vases."

"No, Billy," she said gently. "Squinch up your eyes until they're almost closed and then look."

I did and it was true. They looked like marble. They looked fine and grand. "Oh, Crystal Ball," I said, "I see!"

"I've always had a yearning for marble," she said.

I too have it, and that is why I squinched up my eyes and imagined that Crystal Ball was alive and well and with me at the Mary Kay gala. When you sell plastic that seems like marble you are selling make-believe like Mary Kay sells makeup. They would have understood one another. And Crystal Ball would have gotten a round of applause, the first in her life.

I think a lot about Crystal Ball and how we were raised and how things have changed. We grew up singing hillbilly songs through our noses, and because our roots were rural we grew bored with the reality of the soil and of growing things. In the Dust Bowl nature gave us a living, all right, but it was niggardly. Any kind of contraption that would make life easier was welcome. Nature could be improved upon. The ideal was not something organic but something artificial that could be added. We welcomed engines and chemicals into our garden. Pa preferred the tractor to the mule, the insecticide to the bug. And when the oil boom began, he left the furrow for the drilling rig. The payoff was better and quicker and it got us off the farm and out into what we called the "modren" world.

Ma put away her Mason jars and bought vegetables in cans. We sold the cow and bought milk in bottles. It was a marvel to us that manufacturers could make flowers and plants out of plastic and paneling out of sawdust, that they could make five-and-dime gilt look like Archimedes' gold and sequins look like silver. When our honky-tonk singers put all that glitter on their jeans and boots we thought they were pretty as peacocks. When they were wired for amplification we applauded. It covered up the coarseness. It was like spreading syrup on a biscuit, putting away your work clothes for your Sunday best. Sure, we ran away with ourselves, gooping up everything to the point where even our songs and sermons turned from salt to sugar. Salt was out anyway and refrigeration was in. Maybe it was technology at fault. We lost something in the exchange.

Where once we had been rustics we now became rednecks. Where once we had been provincials hidebound to a time and place, we now became greasy gypsies, moving back and forth across the anticlines of Texas in search of oil. When they put metal houses on wheels and sold them as cheaply as cars we cried Eureka and used them to advantage without any idea that others might be scornful. We took our fundamentalist faith with us, transferring our letter from a small backwoods congregation to that larger, radiating laity of the radio evangelist. We mailed off our offerings to Del Rio and received in return a genuine, simulated photograph-like portrait of Jesus Christ complete with his genuine, simulated autograph. We put it up in a place of honor beside the family Bible and the picture of Crystal Ball with her imitation marble vases.

* * *

But what about the dream woman? In a sense mom, sis, the wife, even the tough little honky-tonk angel, are reachable. What about our woman as the unreachable, the unattainable? Woman as the dream?

I'm going to start with an idea that J. Frank Dobie had about women in relationship to Texas men. Mr. Dobie is dead now. He would have been a hundred years old in 1988. The point is that Dobie, raised on a ranch in Mexican Texas, went back in his blood and cultural memory to the pioneer days. And he saw the settling of Texas and the West as a great masculine adventure. Some women tagged along, and they were resourceful and hardy, of earthly value, but Dobie didn't think they were primary inspirations for their menfolk. The fellows who carved empires down here were romantics, yes, but what turned them on was exploitive adventure. They were pirates in buckskin, swashbucklers and rogues in pursuit of spoils. Dobie said women were necessities to them, not dream figures.

In the Old World, he said, the legends that persisted with the most vitality were legends of women — Venus, Helen of Troy, Dido, Guinevere, Joan of Arc. But in the New World men have been neither lured nor restrained by women. It has been a world of men exploring unknown continents, subduing wildernesses and savage tribes, butchering buffalo, trailing millions of longhorn cattle wilder than buffalo, digging gold out of mountains, pumping oil out of the hot earth beneath the plains. Into this world women have hardly entered except as realities; the idealizations, the legends, have been about great wealth to be found — the wealth of secret mines and hidden treasures, a wealth that is solid and has nothing to do with ephemeral beauty.

Well, I disagree with Pancho Dobie. Yes, most of the men who won power and wealth in Texas were more interested in the things they won than they were in their women. But this is often true of trailblazers. They make lousy lovers and husbands. The woman's man, quiet in his life, often a ne'er-do-well in the eyes of other men, is the cat that gets the cream. And there were, are, more of them with that gleam in their eye than there ever were storied pathfinders. But there were some heroic types almost Old World in their love of woman as some kind of ideal. Sam Houston comes immediately to mind. So does Judge Roy Bean and his fantasy about Lily Langtry.

Now, Pa was no great achiever, just a working man and certainly not much of a lover, but even he had his vision of woman. When we lived out in the chaparral where it seemed that everything was mean and hostile and either pricked or pounced or was poisonous, he liked to observe that the only soft, white things in that whole country were featherbeds and the underbellies of horny toads and women. Even today, in the 59,000-square miles of the Trans-Pecos that isn't taken up by El Paso and a few little towns, there are only four permanent women. Now and then a gal from across the border will traipse across the prairie with something provocative in mind, but they don't last long being passed from hand to hand. A man gets lonesome, and begins to conjure up a woman.

The damndest substitute for a woman I ever saw was an inflatable rubber doll that some old nester out in Presidio County, the hottest place in Texas, had gotten from some smutty mail order house. He paid several hundred dollars for her, blew her up with a tire pump and made love to her for eight years before she ran off with another desert rat. She was life-sized, when aired up, nice and pliable with more-or-less workable parts, and came from the manufacturer with a label and a guarantee. The label said her name was Tina and that she could be washed with a damp, soapy cloth. The guarantee said she was the answer to a hermit's dream and with care she would last longer than most wives and wouldn't cost an arm and a leg to feed. The old codger changed her name to Narcissa McCombs, after some woman who had ditched him in his youth. And he was quite happy with her until the reprobates he played cards with began to get ideas of their own about Narcissa. They fought over her and she chose a fellow from Alamito Creek. My friend was heartbroken, but there was nothing he could do. The woman had made up her mind. She was no longer a dummy. You might think that she could only have been a vacuous, vacant thing, hollow of anything but air, but out there in that lonesome country mirages are as real as clouds and sunsets and shadows, and these old boys had put so much into Narcissa that she took on not only life but a definite character. I'm sure she was the most fetching thing in their lives.

The error they made was grasping for her and trying to realize her. I reckon it's wiser to keep the dream woman at a certain distance. There is something appealing in the art of reserve, especially in this age of suck face. The spectre woman I knew in my youth was just beyond my reach. In fact, she was under glass. And therein lies a tale.

In that time, there were three things to do in Corpus Christi that were worth doing over and over again. Every time Aunt Marguerite and Uncle Herschel came to visit from Cement, Oklahoma, we would take them out to see the seawall, the Driscoll Building and North Beach.

The seawall was an impressive skirt around the city's sea legs, and it was fun to swim from it or fish off the jetties. But we never did those things with Aunt Marguerite and Uncle Herschel. We would take them to the top of the seawall and Daddy would stand and with a sweep of his arm and a rise in his voice he would tell Uncle Herschel just how many tons of cement had gone into the making of the wall. He thought this was of terrible interest to Uncle Herschel because he and Marguerite were from Cement, Oklahoma. Every time they came they got the lowdown on the seawall.

Then we would ride the elevator to the top of the Driscoll Building on the bluff and take in everything from the observation deck. You could see across the bay all the way to Portland. This was as artless a pastime as you could imagine. It was Daddy who managed to bring the risqué to it. He could not resist chortling and telling the story about how Clara Driscoll came to raise the highest building in town. It was low gossip of a high woman, the very regal lady who had saved the Alamo the second time, and Mother hated it, but Pa insisted on reciting it with relish, swearing it was true in every scatological detail when, of course, he had no way of knowing one way or the other. It is sufficient to say that Mrs. Driscoll had been on the bluff first with a building, only to see an arch rival move in next door with an even higher edifice. Swearing that she would someday squat and whiz on the top of the intruder on the bluff, Mrs. Driscoll reached for the sky and built her crowning landmark.

The third attraction was North Beach, the carnival area where my brother and I took music lessons. Once it had been an amusement park for mom and dad and the kiddies, but now, with the war on and the town full of sailors from the naval base, the fun had taken a decidedly adult and seedy turn. There were peep shows and B-girl dives along the strip, con men and crooked games on the midway. You could still roller-skate, dunk the clown and ride the ferris wheel and the bump-a-car, but you had to pick your way through what Mother called a lot of riffraff. She went to North Beach reluctantly, never letting us kids out of her sight. If Pa showed the slightest interest in some gamy tent show, Ma would wheel him around, fasten a child to each of his anchor-like hands, and march her brood out of the park and toward the parking lot and our Terraplane Hudson, vowing never to return. The only way we could lure her back was to talk of cotton candy.

There was one other attraction North Beach offered that women and children could only wonder and whisper about. At the far end of Ocean Drive, just beyond the carnival grounds, an old salt ran a curio shop. The front of the store was open to anyone wanting souvenirs and sea shells, and we spent hours browsing among the bric-a-brac. But the back of the shop was off limits to everyone but men. A giant Chinaman stood guard at the door. He was bald-headed and bare-chested and wore a curving sword in his sash. A fearsome, silent sentinel, ever watchful. Above his head, tacked to the lintel, was a great, carved figurehead of a mermaid, an ornament which once had graced the prow of a clipper. Around her neck hung a hand-painted sign. "Come look upon the Mermaid of Zennor," it read. "See this living siren of the deep in all her natural glory. She lies in a glass aquarium, open to your astounded eyes. She smiles. She sings. She moves her tail. She enters your heart. No man who has ever looked upon the Mermaid of Zennor can ever forget her beauty. $1 for two minutes. $2 for five minutes."

Daddy never went into the Mermaid room with the other men when he was with us, but everyone knew that he went there often with his brother, Uncle Earl. It was something men did that their wives, even Ma, accepted as long as the men didn't talk about it at home. Still, the stories filtered down. There was not a boy in town who did not dream of coming of age and seeing the mermaid. It was a rite, a ritual of manhood, mysterious and wonderfully frightening to anticipate.

It was the next to the last day of summer, the Saturday before school started in August of 1946, that Pa took me aside and told me to get ready, that it was time I saw the Mermaid of Zennor.

I broke into a sweat. "Oh, God," I whispered, "I'm not sure I'm ready, Daddy. I want to, and I don't want to."

"You're fourteen, son. You're ready. You can't put it off. It's something every man has to go through, and you're a new little man. So get ready."

"I thought I had to be twenty-one."

"Naw, stop stalling."

"What do I wear?"

"Wear your Sunday suit and tie."

"Do I have to?"

"Yep, and hurry. Uncle Earl and Uncle Herschel are going with us. They'll be here in a minute."

"Wow! Okay, Pa."

"And Billy, shower and shave."

"Shave? I've never shaved in my life!"

"Damn it, boy. I said shave! Use my razor."

"YESSIR!"

The four of us, very male, handsomely attired and sweetly anointed with Brilliantine, wedged into the Hudson and drove to the curio shop. Daddy splurged. He paid $8 so we could stand over the glass and look at the mermaid for five minutes. I'm not going to tell you what we saw. I'll just say that what the old salt had written on the sign was true. It changed me. It turned me from a boy into a man. This is the first I've spoken of it. Well, once I did confess to my cousin Crystal that the Mermaid of Zennor was the most beautiful creature I had ever seen and that I would remember her until the day I died.

She remains in my mind behind glass, below water. It is such a woman that men at sea and men in the desert summon up. It is such a woman that men lose when they hit port and the oasis. Today, I think, we are in port, sated and suffocated by flesh. With Lily Langtry, Judge Bean never made that mistake.

One night I saw on television a re-run of that old film, "The Westerner," starring Gary Cooper and Walter Brennan. I first saw the movie when I was a kid, and it made an impression on me which held up through adult eyes. Cooper plays a fictitious character, Hardin, a drifter who is brought before Judge Bean for stealing a horse. Of course, Brennan is Roy Bean, and he's about to hang Hardin when Hardin cons him. Hardin notices Lily Langtry's pictures and posters all over the walls of the Jersey Lilly saloon and courtroom, and he tells the judge that not only is he a friend of the famous actress, but that he has a lock of her hair in his gear back in El Paso.

In most of his dealings the old judge is as stingingly skeptical as a vinegarroon scorpion. But when it comes to Lily Langtry, he is a love-struck fool. He wants to hear everything Hardin can tell about Lily. And he wants that lock of her hair Hardin claims to have back in El Paso.

The rest of the story and the other members of the cast are external, and really don't count. They only serve to bring The Law West of the Pecos and the clever cowboy into confrontations which are sometimes friendly, sometimes hostile, and, at the contrived ending, fatal. The scriptwriters have Hardin killing the judge in a gunfight. In real life, Roy Bean dropped dead in his saloon of cantankerous old age (he was over 80) and the wear and tear of too much whiskey. But what I do when I watch the movie is pretend that one day a cowboy did walk into the Jersey Lilly and claim that he had a curl of Miss Langtry's hair. That's what Gary Cooper does. And what Walter Brennan does with Roy Bean is wonderful, makes you think that, yes, this is the way the old judge would have felt and that is exactly what he would have done.

There is one unforgettable scene.

It is when Hardin, back from El Paso, opens his buckskin shirt to pull from his breast the lock of Lily Langtry's hair. By now, you know that Hardin has clipped it from the head of some country girl, but Judge Bean doesn't know it. He watches breathlessly, beside himself with anticipation. The camera moves back. They are out on the range. Behind them, cowboys are rounding up a herd of cattle. You see the desert in the Trans-Pecos, the mountains in the distance, and you have the sense of the hardiness of these men and the loneliness of the land. The camera moves in again. Hardin and Bean are large against the sky. Hardin has a little leather bag in his big hand. He is going to take his time opening it. He is going to drag it out as long as he can. There's a sparkle in his eye which the judge, intent upon the treasure in the sack, does not catch. Hardin begins to tell Judge Bean of the last conversation he had with Lily Langtry.

"Miss Langtry, you plan to go back to England when you finish your American tour?"

" 'No,' she said to me. She said she loved the United States too much. She told me when she was through with the stage she wanted to settle down somewhere in the West, away from all the life of the crowd."

Judge Bean stares in wonder at Hardin.

"She kept asking about Texas. Ever since she was a little girl, she said she had heard about Texas. Always dreamed of Texas. All of her life dreamed of having a home out here."

"She did?" the judge says.

"She did."

Hardin looks at the judge and opens the leather bag. He opens it gingerly, reverently. In the background, you hear a mandolin playing a bitter-sweet, Stephen Foster-like ballad. Hardin reaches in the bag. Judge Bean moans. Hardin pulls from the bag . . . a box. The judge touches his hand to his mouth and gapes. Hardin's eyes twinkle. He has the hair wrapped in paper. He takes off the paper.

"By gosh," the judge whispers.

There it is. Lily Langtry's curl. Hardin knows it really isn't. You know it really isn't. But the judge can only see Lily. You pretend it's Lily's too, and you understand its enchantment for this soiled and bewhiskered old frontiersman.

"Kind of dark, ain't it?" the judge observes.

"She uses a lot of shampoo on her hair," Hardin says.

"She does?"

"She does."

"Beautiful," the judge concludes. He takes the box in his shaking hands and stares at the lock of hair.

"Let me see it," Hardin says, reaching for it.

The judge pulls back.

"Will you?" Hardin insists.

"What fer?" the judge wants to know.

"I ain't gonna keep it."

"I'd like to see you try."

"All right?" Hardin asks.

"All right," the judge says, handing it back.

Hardin touches the curl ever so delicately with his thick forefinger.

"How does it feel, son?" the judge asks. His voice is shaky. He is afraid to touch the lock himself. He is willing for Hardin to have the experience and tell him about it. Besides, he understands how Hardin feels. Hardin is giving up the lock. He won't ever get to touch it again. The judge will have it from here on out. It will be his and his alone.

Later, at the end, just before he is killed, the scriptwriters have Roy Bean meeting Lily Langtry backstage during a performance in San Antonio. It didn't really happen and it doesn't work. The scene with the lock of hair was more than enough. It said everything about dreams and fulfillment.

Lily sang and play-acted in the saloons and honky-tonks of her day and must have thrilled many a Roy Bean heart.

Isn't this part of the reason we go to honky-tonks? We go for fun, yes, to kick up our heels, but behind the gaiety blushes an earnest quest for some other. You never know when she or he (it's the same for the ladies) might glide past your table and catch your eye. For those of us who are happy with the partner we've got, honky-tonking is a great way to keep the magic between you, long as one or the other doesn't stray. How does the old Will Cobb song go?

> Waltz me around again, Willie, around and
> around and around,
> The music is dreamy, it's peaches and
> creamy,
> Oh, don't let my feet touch the ground!

One of the most touching honky-tonk stories I know is that of the granny who wouldn't act her age. She was real and had a name and all that, but I'll just call her Granny. The family's still a bit touchy, though she's been dead for some time now and all the scandal and passion she aroused are buried with her. I'd bet my last dollar on this, though: there's bound to be some truckers, who, when they haul in off the Interstate for a night at the old Flying Crown Club out on I 30 and U.S. 80, lift one to her now and then.

Her survivors would just as soon forget this part of her life. It was, as they say, brief, a kind of crazy wobble to an otherwise decorous and quiet grandmotherhood. And in a sense they are right. Certainly there was nothing in her past to suggest that she would end up doing what she did. They lay it to senility, to a kind of last-gasp gulp for a taste of misspent youth.

She had, of course, been young once, but not wildly so. She had moved from the house of her parents into the house of her husband, had gone from being a child to being a wife and mother and grandmother apparently without ever having a notion to kick up her heels outside the bounds of propriety. If Grandpa had lived she would have faded away as his dutiful and dear companion, and I wouldn't be writing this. But the old gentleman up and died, and Granny, after an appropriate period of mourning, kicked off her old habit and put on such a new face that hardly anyone recognized her.

I saw the change in her, but it didn't distress me the way it did her grandsons and granddaughters. In fact, it kind of tickled me. But then she wasn't my granny. I can see both sides, had to because I sure enough was drawn into it, first by the kids and then by Granny.

One night the oldest grandson, J.D., called me and said, "Billy, will you come and help me persuade Granny to come home?"

"Where is she?"

"The Flying Crown. I hate to tell you, but you'll find out anyway, so you just as well come and help me get her."

That did sound odd. I don't mean that the Flying Crown is not a nice place, even for grannies. It's one of the best country and western clubs this side of Mesquite. It's got a big dance floor, top-notch bands, a responsible and friendly management.

The thing that was odd about it, as far as Granny was concerned, was that it was the last place in the world you'd expect to find her. It is a private club, frequented only by members or guests of the motel in which it is contained, and since mostly truckers stay at the inn and frequent the club, and since Granny had never been known to lay an eye on a trucker, much less hang out with them, it seemed, well, it seemed odd.

There are grannies who dance at the Flying Crown, but they are usually on the arms of their grandpa truckers. Our Granny's grandpa, before he died, was a certified public accountant who was never known to have rolled up his sleeves and honked at anyone.

"J.D.," I said, "I'm on my way."

The lady at the door of the club wouldn't let us in without a membership card, so we had to send a waitress in to tell Granny that we were outside waiting for her.

She came out looking 20 years younger in heels and a gay cocktail dress. She had her a new hairdo, eyes accentuated by makeup. She didn't look gaudy. She looked wonderful. The only thing wrong was that she was obviously embarrassed and close to tears.

"J.D.," she said, "how can you do this to me? You shame me so."

He was embarrassed, too. "I'm sorry, Granny," he said, "but we can't let you do this. I don't want to reflect on your new friends, but we don't know these people and it's not like you to do this sort of thing. I'm here to take you home because we love you and worry about you running around this way at your age."

She looked at him and shook her head. "I may be old, but I'm not a child," she said quietly. "I still live at home alone and take care of myself. If I want to get out a little, after all those years of being cooped up, I ought to be able to do it without causing a family crisis. I've always loved to dance, and you know your grandfather never cared for it. That's all I'm doing, just dancing." Her voice trembled and she stopped. "I came with Sherry. I'll tell her I have to leave. Wait and you can take me home."

"Who is Sherry?" I asked J.D.

"The widow she met at Arthur Murray's," he said. "If it hadn't been for those damned dance lessons, we wouldn't have to put up with this."

"How long has it been going on?"

"Months. She slips off at night like a kid. This is the first time I've had to fetch her. The girls have been dealing with her."

"Does she drink?"

"No, not that we know of."

"Involved with any men?"

"Don't know. Who can say? But even if she doesn't intend to be, she's setting herself up for something bad, hanging out like this. She doesn't know a thing, an innocent really. Sherry seems to be an old hand at this, but, lord, not Granny."

And so it went, back and forth between them with neither side giving in. Granny always went home with them when they found her, but there were nights when she outfoxed them by going to dance halls they didn't know about. They considered having her declared incompetent and their ward, but they couldn't bring themselves to do that. They lived like anxious parents with a wayward kid. I couldn't blame them.

And on the other hand, I couldn't blame Granny, either. I went out with her a couple of times and she was the life of the party. She danced with all the men, even the young ones, and seemed to have the time of her life. Never once did she seem desperate, frantically reaching in the way the kids feared. What she did after the dances were over, if anything, I do not know.

The family wrestled with all sorts of rumors about this man and that; some it was said were young enough to be her grandsons. The talk in itself was scandalous. The only thing for sure was that she made some good friends. The sad thing is that they remained shadowy ones as far as her family was concerned. And she lost them when she got sick and couldn't go out any more. The family gathered around, and she slid back into her old, safe and proper self before she died.

BOOK TWO

The Honky-Tonk States of Texas

On a highway deep within the heart of Texas,
I was just about as lost as I could be.
I was drivin' around in circles
Tryin' to find the border.
Texas was as far as I could see.

Hey, well, I stopped and flagged me
Down a state policeman.
I said my patience was growin' mighty thin.
'Can ye help me get the hell out of Texas?'
He just flashed me some old Lone Star Texas grin
And he said:

'You can't get the hell out of Texas
No matter how hard you try.
Why, in Texas we raised hell, son,
Just like you raise a crop.
It started with the Alamo
And it ain't gonna ever stop.

'As long as there's a Houston and Austin,
Amarillo, Lubbock, Dallas and Fort Worth,
Lord, you can't get the hell out of Texas
Cause it's the hell-raisin' center of the earth!'

"You Can't Get the Hell out of Texas"
by J. Hadley and J. Stafford
recorded by George Jones

CHAPTER 7

The Greatest Honky-Tonk Towns in Texas

Regions

In 1860, I located on the Seco, about forty miles from the town of Bandera, and that is how people came to call me 'Seco' Smith. There were three different Smiths in that region. W. L. Smith lived on the Frio; he was known as 'Frio' Smith. Rube Smith lived on the Hondo; he was called 'Hondo' Smith. I lived on the Seco, and ever since I went there people have called me 'Seco.' These are all Spanish names. In that language, 'frio' means cold, 'hondo' means deep, and 'seco' means dry. I don't know which is more distressing, to be cold, deep or dry.

— *William D. (Seco) Smith*
1836-1926

The dry Seco Creek, when wet, flows into the deep Hondo Creek, and they in their turn flow into the mighty, cold Frio River. All this coming together of elemental extremes is typical of Texas, not only in its lands and waters but in its flora and fauna and certainly in its people. Folks from the outside don't understand this. They think we're all of a piece, just another state in the union. At the risk of sounding smugly provincial, I keep telling them that this is another country, a far country, indeed, and a different people. And I add that even among ourselves we are divided and distinct, and could easily be nine states instead of one. The geography and the climate vary and encourage, often impose, eccentricities that cover us like a caul from birth to death.

The distinctions do not stop with race and national origin. I'm talking about the contrariety of my own people, the wrinkles in us white niggers and white vermin. We may cover the state like a rash, and half of us may soberly pray while the other half drunkenly bray, but even in these passions we beg to differ. Baptists split like cells over the finest points of doctrine and throw up more outlaw congregations than there are honky-tonks in Texas. Now we've come down to the word I want to lay on you, the great truth I learned in my dance across Texas. The urban cowboys in their soft boots did not stomp the home-grown shit and sawdust off our dance floors. They came and made a fancy version of us fashionable, and then they left and we went back to being what we were before, whatever that was in local mien.

A honky-tonk may be a white folks' hangout, but a honky-tonk in West Texas is not a honky-tonk in East Texas. We don't talk the same and we don't dance the same, even when it gets down to asking a lady to two-step. In West Texas there aren't many women to go around, so there's no problem in passing the few from hand to hand at a dance. A stranger can get away with asking someone else's gal to have a whirl, long as it's all copacetic and gentlemanly. You try that in East Texas, where women are so Tyler rose plentiful that picky men grow their own hybrids and hold to them, you'll likely get more than a dirty look. So in the pines bring your own and only let her loose for the Paul Jones and the Cotton-Eyed Joe.

It is a wonder how many versions of the same dance there are, how subtle are the variances and flourishes from town to town, region to region. Everything is so much the same now in America it is a relief to get off the super franchise ruts and see people as almost aboriginal in their manners. It is telling that the closer you get to cities, the more similar the honky-tonk crowd becomes. In the country you do as you please. In the city you conform. The only exception to this I've noticed is among older honky-tonkers. Whether rural or urbanites, they dance with charming naiveté.

Twice in passing I've alluded to the fact that not every redneck is a honky-tonker, but it may surprise you to realize how divided Texas is between wets and drys. Take El Paso to the West, and Orange to the East, and draw a line between them, and you have the border between the drinkers and the teetotalers, each commanding about half the state with the abstainers in the North and the profaners in the South.

At least that's the way it looks on a Texas Liquor Control Board map. But Texas is Texas, friend, and this seemingly deplorable state of affairs has three loopholes in it: moonshine, private clubs and local option. I'm here to say, thirsty brothers and sisters, that in the great and desolate reaches of North Texas where temperance reigns, there are oases, and where there are drinking holes there are honky-tonks. They are out on the highways in wide open, sudden cities like Impact north of Abilene and Gun Barrel City northwest of Athens. These are two of many green-light districts on the fringe of dry areas. And, of course, the larger cities of the upper half of the state usually have gone wet. This has been the trend across the state since liquor-by-the-drink was constitutionally authorized in 1970. Still, if you count county-by-county, a good third of the 254 are dry by law, and most are above the El Paso-Orange line. There are even some dry counties below this curious border. Why the partition? It's a schism as old as God and man, and man and man. They's some that touch the stuff and they's some that don't. They's some that strut their stuff, and they's some that sit and sniff. This cinch on liquor has been called The Bible Belt, but that's unfair to Mexican Catholics and German Lutherans below it who read the Good Book and drink and dance just the same. Of course, it has everything to do with Protestant fundamentalism. The irony is that some of the best honky-tonks are in ostensibly dry country, wet islands in a dry stream.

Before I get on to the honky-tonks themselves, I should remind the reader new to these environs that all this talk about a moral Mason-Dixon severing the state into North and South is applicable only to the spirits in drink. It doesn't designate anything else and certainly doesn't make sense when it comes to the lay of the land and the temper of the people. We are more complex than twins of dueling nature. I don't use the term South Texas and am always reluctant to say North Texas. As I said at the beginning of this section, Texas is at least nine states. To my mind, they are Dallas (i.e. North Texas, if you insist), and, going counterclockwise, West Texas, The Panhandle, The Trans-Pecos, Mexican Texas, The Coast, East Texas, and then, cutting back to the center of the state, the farm country between the Brazos and Colorado, and The Hill Country. These regions are not entire unto themselves for nothing. I mean I'm not being arbitrary. They exist physically and metaphysically, and I was pleased to see that the phone company came close to understanding this when they drew the lines for the area codes. They make 806 and the Panhandle dip down too far into West Texas, and they screw up by making 817 and Ft. Worth look like North-Central Texas. Then 214 and Dallas is dumped in with East Texas, while 713 and Houston and The Coast are pulled up short before they reach Corpus Christi. I'd say that 512 and Mexican Texas is almost correct. It shouldn't include Austin and The Hill Country and the lower coast. And out in 915 they don't mark the difference between the Trans-Pecos and West Texas. I'd give them a B- on six out of eight, and an F on the blanks they drew with the Hill Country, the farm country, and the Trans-Pecos.

* * *

I remember one time we were coming down off the High Plains of West Texas when Daddy pulled the car off the road outside of San Angelo and said, "See that little road going off out yonder?"

"Yessir."

"Well, if we drive out to where it quits, we'll be right smack dab in the center of Texas."

Sure, enough, we drove out Farm Road 1233, and sure enough it petered out in the middle of the sand hills of Tom Green County. Daddy got out and dug his shoes into the sand at the end of the pavement. Proudly, he stood there, and gave us a lecture on the dead reckoning required for accurate topography and topology. It went something like this:

"Everything in Texas is catawampus."

The gravity and magnetic forces list to starboard, and so do our notions. Look at a map of the Lone Star State. Austin was deemed the state capital because it was perceived as being at the center of the state and the population. Neither was nor is true. Anyone who's been out of the rarified air and magnetic field of Texas for one minute can look back and realize that Austin in Travis County is not anywhere near the heart of the state. It's off to the right, about the middle of the right, and it's low right, edging into the mesquite and *patrón-peon* country.

Actually, there are two centers of the state far to the left of Austin which are not recognized or even whispered about. One is the eyeball bull's-eye. It is in a field of cow patties and oil wells between Camp San Saba and Camp Air, just barely in Mason County two miles south of bordering McCulloch County. But if you pick up a sextant and a gyrocompass and measure distance and latitude and longitude, you have to say that the real center of Texas is the petered-out end of Farm Road 1233 where Daddy stood. It is 20 miles southeast of San Angelo.

No one wanted to put the state capital in such forlorn places, at least no one important enough to have a say-so. What they did was pull out their witching sticks and declare, like daft Copernicuses, that Austin was the actual and celestial core of community and civics. Things have been cockeyed ever since.

CHAPTER 8

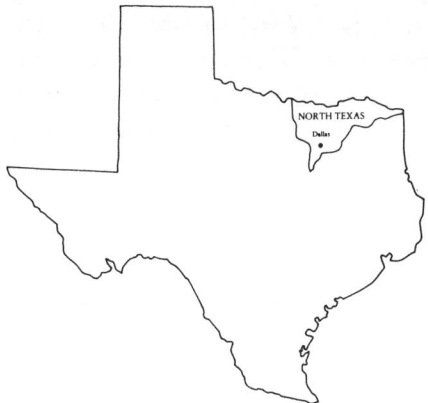

Dallas (aka North Texas): A Strange Oasis

Except for its honky-tonks, Dallas doesn't belong to Texas. And if we insist on consistency of character, Dallas shouldn't have honky-tonks. Religious fundamentalism is as faithful to Dallas' nature as finance, finery and football. There are flamboyant possibilities in each, and yet Dallas, as rich and well-dressed and winning as it is, has seldom had a flair for the extremes. Our most recent defection, in the '50's and '60's, was of a political nature and of such tragic import that we moved immediately back, like Greeks in retreat from hubris, toward moderation in all things. We have tended to worship God and mammon and gowns and games with a certain highly efficient reserve. This is no way to honky-tonk.

Look at the transformation of that Jolly Roger known as Staubach. At Navy he ran amok like a possessed Pentecost, throwing miracles into the end zone with such divine regularity that fans came to believe that each Saturday he would indeed turn the water of the earth into the wine of heaven. Later, in Dallas, we did not expect that of him. Under the Cotton Mather Puritanism of Tom Landry, Roger was exorcised of his creative demons and played with cool, calculating professionalism. In ecclesiastical terms, he had moved from being a shouting Shaker to a restrained and reasoning Episcopalian. This is metaphor, of course. Roger is really a Catholic. Landry is a Baptist. The point is that Dallas turned Staubach, as a football player, from his heart to his head. This is no way to honky-tonk.

This Dallas tendency toward abstraction is even evident in the place it has on the map. North Texas is a misnomer. If the West begins in Fort Worth and goes as far north as Vernon and as far south as Junction, and if the western edge of East Texas starts on a northern curve that goes down from Texarkana through Sulphur Springs, Corsicana and Bryan and Huntsville, where in Heaven's name does that leave North Texas? It leaves it in a tight little squeeze of conjecture between the Elm and East forks of the Trinity, I.H. 30 and the Red River. The only cities you might throw in there with Dallas are Greenville, Sherman, Denison, Paris and Clarksville. Mostly country of sober rectitude. No place to honky-tonk.

But this is the incredible thing: for all this angst over decorum, the queen city of the North has as many good honky-tonks as any town in Texas. Yes, I'm talking about Dallas! I know it's hard to believe. This in a community where, not long ago, a Southern Methodist chaplain was ostracized after he danced down the aisle with the bride of a couple he had just married. But, thanks to precinct choice and a joy of life even in Cold City, we have our Bacchanalia, C&W style.

These are her honky-tonks, among many, that I and thousands of others find special:

THE LONGHORN BALLROOM
216 Corinth at Industrial
Dallas

One of the great dance halls, long standing, traditional with no mechanical bulls and gimmicky b.s. A legendary place to take your lady, and it's all because of Dewey Groom. Groom not only owns the ballroom, he sings and leads the house band and always introduces the stars who are booked in every week. From April through June we danced to David Frizzell, Joe Stampley, Gene Watson, Earl Thomas Conley and Delbert McClinton. The Longhorn attracts young and old, rich and workingman, even entertainers on their night off. Mell Tillis, Willie Nelson, and even Mick Jagger, have been known to drop in for a brew when passing through. And, again, the reason is Dewey Groom and his good family who make everyone feel at home.

You can't miss the honky-tonk. Its enormous Ballroom sign, with a twenty-one-foot steer, is a Dallas trademark. A sprawling club with a big dancefloor (6,000 square feet), its facade is duded up to look like a western town with 21 storefronts, lit at night by 3,000 lights. My favorite scene outside is the giant Texas map showing the hometowns of all the country music stars.

Remember when you used to drive into Dallas and see those big signs that read: "O. L. Nelms thanks Dallas for helping him make another Million!"? It was eccentric Mr. Nelms who built the Longhorn Ballroom in 1950 for Bob Wills. Wills fiddled with it for a while and then backed off because of tax problems. Managers came and went, including Jack Ruby and Dewey Groom. But Dewey returned in 1958 to rent the place, which had closed. He poured

$350,000 of his own money into the Longhorn and started booking the biggies: Roy Acuff, Moon Mullican, Webb Pierce, Jim Reeves, Carl Smith, Ernest Tubb, Kitty Wells, Bob Wills. Before he died, Nelms paid Groom back for all his money and trouble by giving him the property, now appraised at five million dollars.

The Longhorn is open Wednesday through Sunday for dancing. The band starts at 8:30 p.m. on weekdays and 9 p.m. on weekends. Sunday matinee doors open at 5 p.m. and the band kicks off at 6. Free country dance lessons from 7 to 8 on Wednesday and Thursday nights. No one under 19 allowed, but Dewey's sons and daughter work at the Longhorn, keeping it in the tradition of the family honky-tonk.

* * *

A place as storied as the Longhorn Ballroom has its legends, and one of the best tales I ever got there was about the Midnight Dancer, a regular customer during the early Sixties.

He was, they say, a good-looking little devil, built slender-hipped and compact like a flamenco dancer, and of course he was light on his feet and sure-handed with his partner. Any woman who ever danced with him said he was without question the best. He had a way of holding his lady that was subtly elegant but difficult to describe. Other men would imitate him but it was never quite the same. One woman said it was because he held her with his eyes as much as he did with his arms, and that he maintained a distance between his body and hers that was somehow more provocative than being pressed up close by a sweating hugger. But the best thing about him was his restraint, his reserve. He never showed you everything, not on the dancefloor and certainly not at the tables over a beer. He came and went like a phantom, and even today, years after his death and all the talk about the circumstances surrounding the discovery of his body, the mystery remains.

Don Guillermo del Campo is all they knew to call him, apparently at his insistence. Although that name now seems to have been one of his affectations, it fit at the time. It means, in rough translation, Sir William of the Country. He was, to the dance hall ladies, the very incarnation of a Latin lover, Valentino-style. He showed up every night of the week at a different ballroom on the Southside. He was in Oak Cliff a lot, and occasionally he would venture across the Trinity and make the Longhorn Ballroom on Industrial. These were always country-western places frequented by middle-aged Anglos, most of them working men and waitresses and such, which means that his flamboyant dress accentuated his difference. He always wore black — a low crowned, broad-brimmed, black hat, a tight-fitting black shirt with full sleeves, tight, black pants flared below the knees, and shiny black boots with unusually high heels.

"What made him such a legend?" I asked this Oak Cliff woman the other day. She is old now, retired from slinging scrambled eggs at the Lucas B&B, resigned to the fact that her dancing days are over, but her eyes lit up when she began to talk about Don Guillermo. For a reason that will be apparent, she insisted that I not use her name.

"It was everything about him," she said. She paused and lit a cigarette, took some time to collect her thoughts. "Of course," she began again, "the main thing was his dancing. Most of the men who hang out at honky-tonks tend to jerk your arm off and mash your corns. Don Guillermo was divine. If he ever stepped on a toe I never heard about it. All he ever did was slow dance, and he never got fancy. You know, he never tried to show off. And yet you knew he had it in him to blow everybody off the floor. You knew that if he ever decided to let loose he had the moves. But he always kept himself in check. It built up the tension and made his dancing exciting.

"Another thing was his mystery. He never said much, never said where he was from or what he did for a living. You never knew when he would show up or where. He seldom made the same place more than once a month, although you knew he was out dancing every night. You'd hear that he was at so-and-so's. Some of us girls would try to anticipate him, tried to guess where he'd be on a certain night and catch him there, but it seldom worked.

"I'll be frank with you, long as you don't identify me. I don't mind admitting that I tried several times to get him to take me home with him, or let me take him home with me, but he always politely declined. He could say no in a way that didn't insult you. It also made you feel better knowing that you weren't the only woman who'd ever made a move on him and failed. God, we all stood in line! As far as I know, he never took any one of us up on it.

"He just came to dance, and it was magic. He arrived late, around 10, and never stayed much past midnight, but in that couple of hours he danced us off our feet and carried away our hearts. Then he was gone, just like that! We didn't even know how he came and went, whether he had a car or whether someone drove him. As far as we knew, he just materialized out of thin air. You figured he was middle-aged, but there was something eternally youthful about him. His hair and his moustache were black and shiny as the leather on his boots, and he didn't have an ounce of fat on him. He stayed this way for years while all the rest of us were showing the wear and tear. He was, well, he was like a movie star who never grows old."

It was on a wintry night, several years ago, that they found his body in a cheap motel out on U.S. 77 just past Red Bird Airport. No foul play. He had died in bed of a heart attack, apparently after coming in from a dance because he still had his black outfit and boots on. The motel people said he'd been staying there off and on for years, that he paid for his room in the name of Clyde Curlee, and that that was about all they knew, that he was a loner who kept to himself. He had no driver's license or any kind of identification by which the authorities could trace his origin or kin, though they did find enough cash to give him a decent burial.

The astonishing thing was that the undertaker who prepared the body said that Mr. Curlee, or Don Guillermo, was easily a man in his late 70's, maybe even into his 80's. He was in good shape, to be sure, save for the heart that failed him all of a sudden, but he was definitely up in years. His hair and moustache, even his eyebrows, were dyed, and he wore makeup to cover up the wrinkles. In his closet hung another black outfit, a replica of the one he had on when they found him, that and a couple of shirts and jeans. That was it. The only clue to his past was a tantalizing scrap that had been torn from some newspaper story and carried in his billfold until it had yellowed. Only a line or two could be made out, but it was something about a Curlee having been a stunt man out in Hollywood during the 20's and 30's. I picked up that thread and tried to follow it, but it led nowhere.

PALMS DANCELAND
4906 Military Parkway
Dallas

The Palms Danceland is known as the "pressure cooker" because so many wives of workingmen hang out there during the day and then rush home to whip up a meal before hubby gets home. Well, there's more to Danceland than that, but still it's best not to go snooping around like a private eye. It is a fascinating place to while away the days when you're working nights. The Palms is open from 9 a.m. to 5 p.m., Monday through Friday. Men pay $2 at the door, unescorted ladies enter free. There's a neon sign out front over the concrete brick building which burns in the daylight, and on the inside the club is very dark, for good reason. Manager Donna Carter admits the crowds are strange. "It's a real mixed bag," she says. "We get housewives, people on their lunch break, cowboys, young people, old people. On the average we'll see a hundred people in and out in a day, and on Thursdays and Fridays we'll have six hundred."

Palms Danceland has been on Military Parkway for 25 years, owned by Joe Perryman. The odd hours and clientele have drawn attention to the place. It's been featured on "That's Incredible," "Phil Donahue," and in national magazines. "It's getting to be a tourist attraction," one regular said nervously. "Even a woman from West Germany walked in here one day." No minors allowed. Check camera at the door. Texas Tequilla plays every day.

DEBONAIR DANCELAND, INC.
2810 Samuel Blvd.
Dallas (On corner of Samuel and Winslow)

Here is another dance hall where the owners are also band-members. Earl F. Martin (lead guitar) and Don W. McKnight (bass and vocals) started out at

Palms Danceland years ago. The third owner of the Debonair, James H. Coltharp, hired them to play the Southern Club (which he owned) and eventually bought the Debonair. Earl and Don play with the Debonairs on separate nights of the week, but their regular customers have learned when to come. The Debonair is roomy — it can seat 1,000 — and with a twenty-year legacy, the (original) Debonairs can play some great tunes. You have to be 19 to get in, but after that the crowd is mixed. They work really hard to make it a homey place to have a few drinks and tap to some great country music. Hours are Monday through Saturday, 1 p.m. to 2 a.m., Sunday, 2 p.m. to 2 a.m. The band starts at 8 p.m. every night.

Floyd Berry is deceptive. When he's with Ivy Dale at Debonair Danceland he's just another good old boy, though he is rather tall and stately with the waltz. You would never know he's something of a scholar (self-taught) and an artist. Floyd paints horses. I don't mean he slops latex all over stolen steeds. His medium is acrylic on canvas and horses are his subject. Every weekend before the first Monday of the month, he and Ivy Dale take a load of Floyd's paintings in their van and sell them at the trade fair in Canton. Ivy Dale would rather honky-tonk than anything else, but once in awhile Floyd will elevate her, as he calls it, with a visit to the Dallas Fine Arts Museum. Not long ago, Floyd and Ivy Dale went to the musuem for a special exhibition. This is what transpired.

"Floyd, leave that alone," Ivy Dale said, an edge in her voice.

"I'm not doin' nothin'," he said in a whisper, looking back at the guard.

"You were too," she said, raising her voice too loudly to suit him. "I saw you touch it with your dirty old finger."

"I just wanted to know how it felt," he roared under his breath.

"Land sakes," she whined. "Let's go before they throw us out. That painting you touched must be worth umpteen million dollars. Not that it's worth it, mind you. I don't know why you wanted to come in the first place. I'm cockeyed if I see why they make such a fuss over Mel Greeko. Shoot, Floyd, I like your paintings better."

"That's because you're ignorant, Ivy Dale. A dabbler like me can't hold a candle to a master like that. And it's El Greco, not Mel Greeko."

Ivy Dale looked at her husband ferociously. "Try to pay the fool a compliment and he insults you," she muttered.

They left the museum and walked to the parking lot.

"Ivy Dale, you drive," Floyd said. "I want to think about what I saw." He leaned back in the passenger seat, closed his eyes, and seemed to fall into a deep reverie.

"Floyd, you ain't fooling me," Ivy Dale said. "You ain't thinking about art and Mel Greeko and all such as that. You're thinking about the fried chicken and peach cobbler I said I'd have for supper."

"Hush up, woman! Give a man some peace. I like your cooking, and you know I like it when you really cook and don't zap everything in the microwave. I like your cooking better'n anything, but you can't compare fried chicken and peach cobbler to something like the 'Baptism of Christ' or 'Mary Magdalene in Penitence.' Sometimes I don't think there's a brain in your head."

"Well, I may not be up on your hoity-toity art, and know all the names of Mel Greeko's paintings and everything, but I tell you this, Floyd Dwayne Berry, I got enough sense not to walk up to one of his paintings in broad daylight and touch it with my finger!"

"Ivy Dale, you don't know why I did it. You ought to know that before you start stickin' *your* finger at me. It's wrong, yes. But I did it because I was in El Greco's power. He had a hold of me and drew me to touch his figure of Christ, just as he himself had touched it many times. You know that, Ivy Dale? He used to run his fingers all over his paintings to give them the feel and color of his own sweat and flesh. Three hundred and seventy years ago, El Greco touched that painting, and I did it today. I guess if everyone who's seen it had done that it'd be wore out. That's why they got guards. But I just couldn't help myself."

"Floyd?"

"Huh?"

"What were those machines with the little ink needles on them? You know, the ones under some of the paintings?"

"I asked the guard," Floyd said, "and he said they were to gauge humility."

"You mean they record people's reaction to the paintings?"

"I guess so."

"Lord," Ivy Dale laughed. "I guess I flunked. Wasn't properly appreciative. No wonder the guards were so humorless. But I'm sure you more than made up for me."

They rode in silence.

After awhile, Floyd stirred himself. "Ivy Dale," he said earnestly, "I've got to stop painting horses and do something more ambitious."

"Horses are what sells at Canton."

"Yeah," he said, sighing. "Mel Greeko sure wouldn't sell well at First Monday." Then he started laughing.

"What's gotten into you?" Ivy Dale asked.

"That was funny, you calling him Mel Greeko. In an awful way, you were right. He was Greek. His name was Theo-to-kop-oulos, something like that, so the Spanish called him 'El Greco,' which just means 'The Greek'."

Ivy Dale smiled. "They were just folks too."

"Yeah," Floyd said, grinning. He patted her plump little thigh and thought of drumsticks.

FRONTIER
9716 Harry Hines Blvd.
Dallas

Another one of Joe Perryman's solid establishments (Palms Danceland), the Frontier is not much of a place to look at (red wallpaper, black chairs) but the regulars wouldn't leave it for the world. Stallion plays Tuesday through Saturday to a mostly young crowd. There are video machines, pool tables and lots of drink specials. But don't get the idea that Frontier is a Texas Chic Johnny-come-lately. It's been on Harry Hines for ten years and has at least that much more to go.

THE OLD SADIE HAWKINS
2515 W. Jefferson
Grand Prairie

When Red and Margie Blassingame first opened up the Old Sadie Hawkins club, they barely had a dime to their names. They had run the Old Colonial Club, and after it burned, they scraped together all they had and built Sadie's. There was only a concrete floor and ladder-back chairs then, and plywood tables that first night twenty years ago, but when Red and Margie opened the door, they couldn't believe their eyes. The parking lot was full of folks waiting to get inside.

Sadie's has been remodelled since then, but Katy, a bartender there for six years, says she wouldn't let them change the bar. "It's great in here," she said. There's plenty of footrailing and a good dance floor. It's one of twelve bars in a shopping center, but Katy says her customers "don't even know there's another bar in Texas." Nobody's Band plays Wednesday through Sunday. At night the crowd is young, and during the day it's older (hours are from noon to 2 a.m.) and some real cowpeople wander in sometimes. Katy says nearly everyone out in Grand Prairie is country, and they must be, because now Red and Margie are millionaires. Their place is one of the favorite hangouts for the professor of honky-tonks, Dr. James Ward Lee.

The Greatest Honky-Tonks in Texas

The Broken Spoke, Austin, may be one of the only dance halls anywhere with a citation from the State Legislature commending its services. Owner James White, above, is duly proud.

Jay Godwin

Floore Country Store and Dance Hall in Helotes, Texas claims the honor of launching, among others, singer Willie Nelson. Papa Joe and wife Estella run one of the most popular outdoor cantinas and dance halls in the state.

Jay Godwin

Crider's Cafe, near Hunt, Texas in the Hill Country, is owned and operated by brothers Gene and Wilton Crider, above, and Wilton's wife Bobbie Nell. In addition to great home-cooked meals, the emporium features outdoor dancing, a rodeo, and swing bands of the Bob Wills variety.

Gruene Hall, in the village of Gruene, Texas northeast of New Braunfels, the largest German-settled area in the state, is billed as the oldest dance hall in Texas, and hasn't gone a week without a dance since opening around the turn of the century.

Jay Godwin

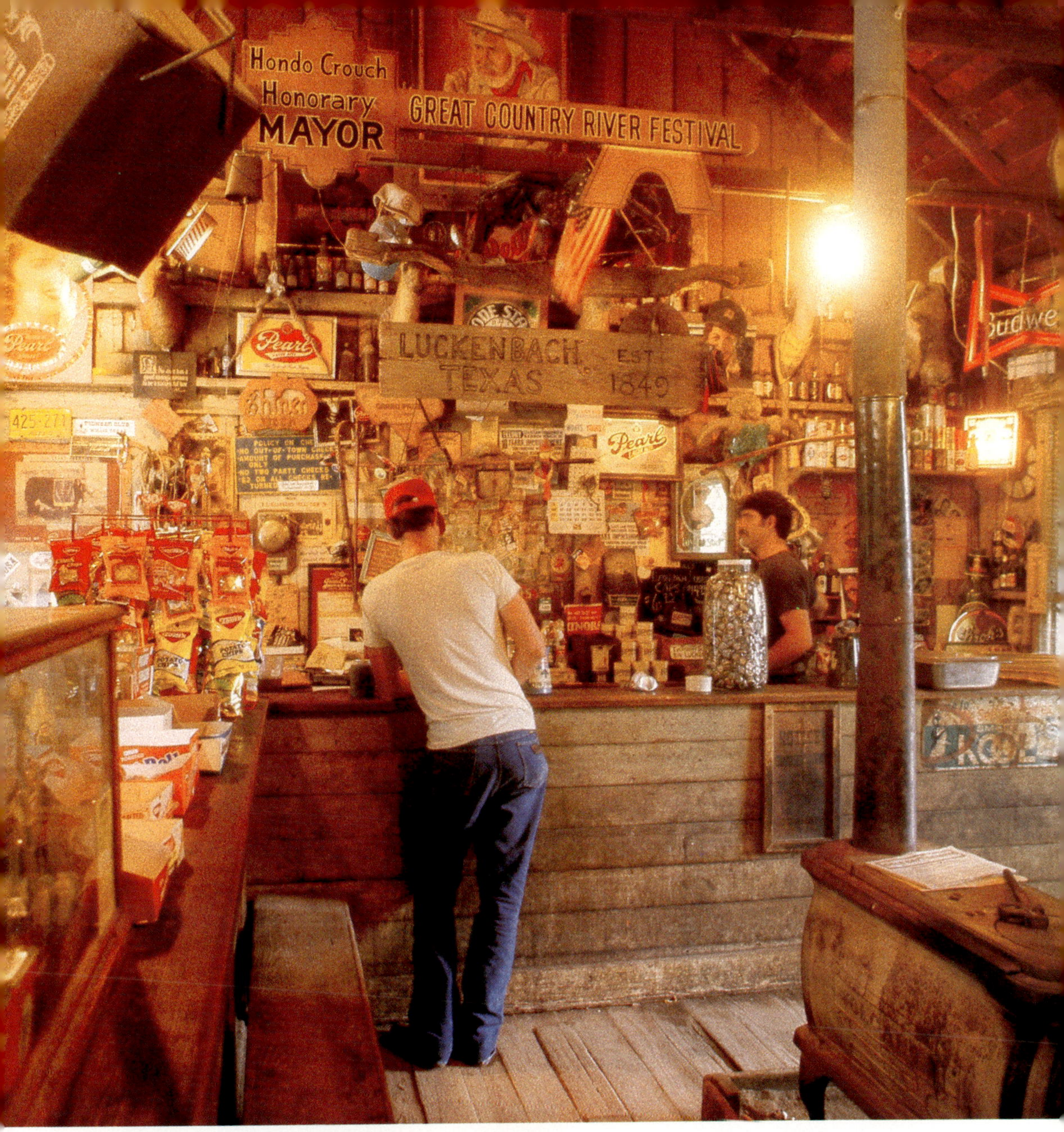

Jay Godwin

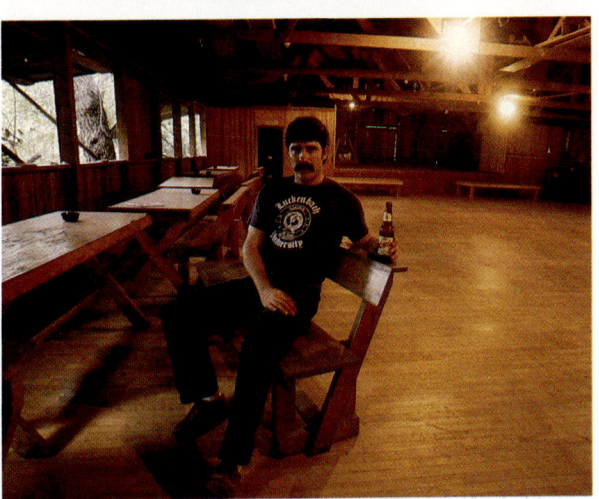

Luckenbach Dance Hall and Store, hailed in song and legend, has enjoyed prime-time exposure and still attracts thousands of visitors to this tiny Hill Country town. The enormous dance hall, a chili cookoff, and frequent visits from name entertainers are managed by Becky and Cris, daughters of the late, great Hondo Crouch.

The Texas Star Inn, located on the Bandera Road near San Antonio, is a genuine Texas honky-tonk even by a purist's standards. Overseen by Dodie Sullivan and Polly Herschberger, the Texas Star features live music, dance lessons, and home cooking. Parts of *Waltz Across Texas* were filmed here.

Gilley's in Houston is still one of the top places in Texas for ropers, Rexall Rangers, and tourists alike. Mickey's bouncer and bodyguard, known as Killer, keeps an eye on things while the infamous bullride, the video arcade, pool tables and carnival atmosphere keep the fans enthralled. Urban cowboys and dudes alike can take a turn on the club's enormous dancefloor.

Timothy Bullard

Evans Caglage

Evans Caglage

Billy Bob's Texas, in Fort Worth, is the biggest of its kind anywhere. Owners Billy Bob Barnett and Spencer Taylor run the largest honky-tonk in the world, featuring forty-two bar stations, a western store, three restaurants and a rodeo on weekends. The club presents top C&W entertainment.

The Pickin' Parlour on Fort Worth's old Northside, a whiff away from the famed Stockyards and Rodeo Grounds, is a favorite haunt of characters like Steve Murren, above right, dubbed "The Mayor of Northside." The club's Miss Kitty style decor and house band, Hill City, draw in traffic from the boardwalk.

Evans Caglage

Evans Caglage

The Longhorn Ballroom, just off the Corinth Street viaduct in old South Dallas, is one of the great legendary places of the Southwest. Owner Dewey Groom leads the house band and welcomes such name talent as Mel Tillis, Willie Nelson, Joe Stampley and Jerry Jeff Walker to capacity crowds.

Evans Caglage

Palms Danceland on Military Parkway in East Dallas is one of an odd assortment of Texas honky-tonks frequented by a daytime crowd of cowboys, playboys, and workingmen's wives while the 9 to 5 crowd goes its own way. After twenty-five years in the business, the Palms has been featured on "That's Incredible," "Phil Donahue," and in national magazines.

Evans Caglage

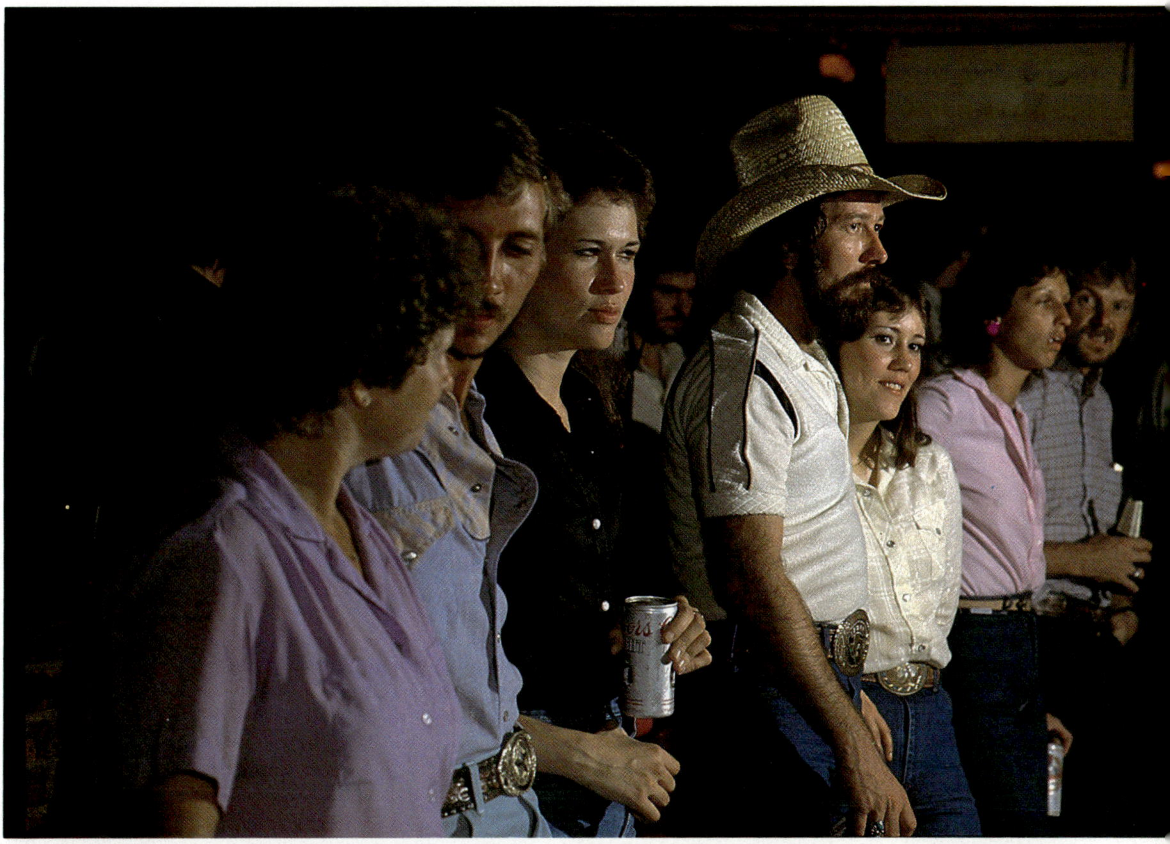

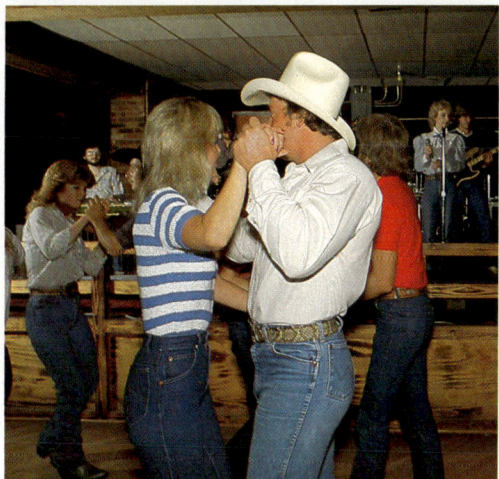

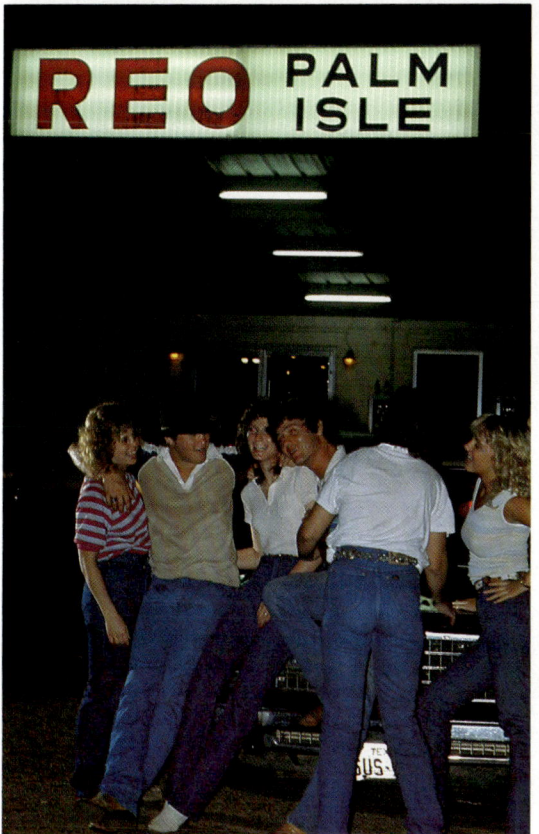

The Reo Palm Isle in Longview, Texas has been rated by AP as the best club in the state. Owner Carl Johnson has hosted celebrities and tourists, including CBS news, for a taste of East Texas' special brand of honky-tonk entertainment.

The Caravan East, El Paso, is a cut above the typical wayside honky-tonk, with cover charge and a better than average dress code, and opulent surroundings. The club draws top C&W entertainment.

Carlos Rosales

Schroeder Dance Hall, located fifteen miles from the town of Goliad in South Texas, is a weekends-only honky-tonk managed by owner Byron Hoff. The colorful sign out front and the modest exterior barely disguise this classic roadhouse, where young and old are equally welcome.

W. G. Roberts

Henry Bargas

The Caravan East, Amarillo, is capped by the largest sign in town, 60 feet long by 20 feet high and surrounded by some 488 lights. The equally extravagant club features 12,000 square feet of carpeted floor space, with chandeliers, and brings in top talent like the Bellamy Brothers, Brenda Lee and Louise Mandrell. Open seven nights, it's always SRO.

CHAPTER 9

West Texas

Fort Worth: The Gateway

From the beginning there was between Dallas and Fort Worth a kind of hyperbolic squaring off, in strong language and deed, of two very different peoples and places. The thirty-three miles that separated them were, in John Gunther's words, a chasm as definitive as the Continental Divide. One senses it still, even in the obvious way the country changes. Dallas is softer, shady, an edge of East Texas. Fort Worth has a bigger sky, is a little hotter in the summer, colder in the winter, drier and higher. The West. Dallas is city; Fort Worth country. Visitors like Cowtown. Big D tries too hard. From the beginning, Fort Worth was appealing because it was on the edge of the frontier, big enough to be comfortable and white-man-safe but close enough to the wide open spaces to be exciting. There was a string of saloons and whorehouses called Hell's Half Acre. Butch Cassidy hid out there. Quanah Parker, the last chief of the Comanche, made Fort Worth his home off the reservation, and Teddy Roosevelt came to ride and hunt. And there was no better place to honky-tonk. The cattle drives brought cowboys to the stockyards, and thence to the saloons, and when they struck oil on the plains the roughnecks came to throw away their money in the dives along the Jacksboro Highway, still a flavorful strip to honk your tonk.

After a heavy Mexican meal at Joe T. Garcia, you can shed some calories by dancing. Here are the places that have worn out my tamale:

BILLY BOB'S TEXAS
2520 N. Commerce
(Fort Worth Stockyards)
Fort Worth

Owners Billy Bob Barnett and Spencer Taylor have made their club the biggest honky-tonk in the world. There are 42 bar stations, a retail western store, three restaurants and a rodeo on Friday and Saturday nights. (Just for real cowboys.) They feature live bands every night, drawing some of the biggest stars in C&W. The house band is Texas Pride and they deserve the name. They are great. One disturbing note for the purists. Billy Bob's has started booking in rock 'n' roll acts between the country. Still, Billy Bob's is the wildest attraction in Fort Worth since Amon Carter hired Billy Rose and Sally Rand to head up the 1936 Texas Frontier Centennial, Cowtown's answer to the official Texas Centennial and State Fair which opened at the same time in Dallas. Dallas drew the most visitors, but Fort Worth's centennial was popular and the most publicized, mainly because Carter brought in a thousand newspaper columnists from around the country. Damon Runyon quipped, "In Dallas the women wear high heels. In Fort Worth men do."

Well, Cowtown is still a stepper's town and the Gateway to the West, and Billy Bob's is headquarters for whoopee. The club has only been open since April, 1981, but already it has a reputation huge enough to survive off tourists, let alone the locals. But that isn't enough. Barnett and Spencer are expanding the club. Already, there's too much to see and do in just one night. It's a must if you're ever in Fort Worth, and seems on its rollicking way to becoming a fixture like Angelo's barbecue, Massey's chicken-fried steak and Joe T. Garcia's Mexican food.

PICKIN' PARLOUR
103 W. Exchange
Fort Worth

There are lots of dancing bars on West Exchange in Fort Worth, but the Pickin' Parlour is the only one you can see into from the street. Looking in the plate glass windows in the front you might see a lot of people and a lot of animal heads on the wall. As manager Robin Perkins puts it, "It's decorated Miss Kitty style." There are ceiling fans and beer signs and a house band called Hill City. You might find the Mayor of Northside (dubbed by his drinking buddies) at the bar Tuesday through Saturday from 5 p.m. to 2 a.m. Biggest competition is Cowtown U.S.A.

COWTOWN U.S.A.
120 W. Exchange
Fort Worth

This place kind of says it for Fort Worth. It's been there "a long time," say the folks who dance there. It's brick on the outside with a long porch like an old pioneer house. Inside there's a wooden dance floor for any of the 150 patrons who can fit through the doors. There's live music Wednesday through Saturday nights and a DJ on Sundays. Young crowd.

* * *

Bob Wills and Aunt Earline

You can't leave Fort Worth without a tip of the hat to the memory of The King of Western Swing, Bob Wills. So much of Wills' early career was staged there, beginning with those house parties and Wills' Fiddle Band. Later, he and his boys were the Aladdin Laddies on WBAP, the Fort Worth Doughboys and the Light Crust Doughboys on KFJZ. In my own mind I always associate Bob Wills with my Aunt Earline, who dropped me a card just the other day.

Earline writes from Evening Shade, Arkansas, that one of her boarders sat down on her most prized Bob Wills record, the one he made with Merle Haggard just before Wills died, and busted the bejesus out of it. The poor woman is disconsolate, encloses 10 bucks and a plea for me to please go out and find her another copy of "For The Last Time," and mail it to her posthaste.

Well, I'm happy to say that the album is already on its way to the Ozarks. I've been to Evening Shade. I know how boring it can get, even if you're a good-looking old gal running a boarding house full of drifters. Once in awhile, Earline gets a wild hair and hauls off and drives over to Bald Knob or Thayer, the two nearest towns, but mostly she sits on a bar stool in her kitchen polishing her fingernails and drinking beer and smoking cigarettes and playing country music on the radio or the record player, maybe jawing with one of her good-ol-boy roomers, while waiting for the ever-present whole haunch-of-a-steer roast in the oven to cook. No matter how big and bawling a hunk of meat she serves up for supper, it is reduced to a bone or two by the time the men leave the long table. Such carnivorous appetites you have never seen. Earline says they'd eat the hooves and tail if she put such as that in front of them.

If you're ever passing through that part of the country, drop in and see old Earline. She'll give you a meal you won't forget, and a room for the night you'd just as soon forget. As a hostess she doesn't put a lot of effort into the amenities. If a pipe breaks, she wraps it in gaff tape. If a roach or a rat runs across the floor, she'll take aim and try to spear it with a high-heeled shoe.

But there's always cold beer and Bob Wills. She plays his old records day and night without letup, at such volume you can hear it in an upstairs bedroom with your ears stuffed with cotton wadding and a pillow over your head. And if you look like you can do the Texas Two Step or Betty's Waltz, she'll come down off that stool and dance you ragged.

I feel kind of sorry for her. None of the clods she drags around the floor nowadays are anywhere near up to Uncle John. When I see her locked into some galoot's arms, her head on his chest and her eyes rolled back in her head like some blissful cow, I know she's really gone back to Rob's Place in Robstown, Texas. Bob Wills and the Texas Playboys are swinging up on the bandstand, and Uncle John, tall, sweet-talking, smooth-dancing Uncle John, is pulling her around and around making her dizzy in a way that liquor can never do.

It's funny. The last time I saw the three of them in their prime — I mean Earline and John and Bob Wills — was at a country dance in Yorktown, Texas. It must have been the summer of 1949. Uncle John was working derricks on a big steam rig, and he got me on as a morning tour roughneck for the summer. Yorktown was German Bohemian country. Every other establishment on the square was a beer hall, and on Saturday nights everyone came from miles to dance at a big pavilion on the edge of town. On this particular Saturday, John and I had to report to the rig before midnight, but we got Earline and went stomping anyhow because Bob Wills and the Playboys were playing.

We had seen Wills in the movies, had heard him and the old Light Crust Doughboys on the radio, and we had seen him at many a dance, so he was as familiar to us as any famous star, only much more comfortable and neighborly. Hell, he was just an old country boy, too, raised in Turkey, Texas, over in Hall County. He always wore a little belly over his sagging belt, a cigar in the corner of his mouth, and that 10-gallon white hat. And, of course, he carried his fiddle. He never looked flashy, never wore any of that stupid spangle, looked like he had put on starched dress khakis to walk down to the town square and pass the time of day. The only thing expensive about him was that cowboy hat, which must have cost a hundred, and maybe his boots.

When he walked up to the microphone to start the dance, he always said the same thing:

"Howdy, everybody from near and far. You want to know just who we are? We're the Texas Playboys from the Lone Star..."

The fiddles would start to sing and the music would not let up, would not let you rest. You couldn't not dance. If there weren't enough men to go around, women danced with women. I remember that during the break that night, Bob Wills stepped down into the crowd to have a beer, and Earline went up to him and gave him a big kiss. He hugged her, called her "Little Lady," and shook hands with John and me and asked us what we'd like to hear in the next set.

He'd already played "San Antonio Rose" and all those lyrical tunes that Tommy Duncan and Leon McAuliffe sang so well. So Earline asked him to play the rags, "Texas Playboy," "Lone Star," "Wills Breakdown."

Well, when the band returned, they broke into it, and Earline and John pumped and jigged around that huge hall for all they were worth. They danced everybody off the floor but a couple of diehards, and when it was over they got a big hand, and Bob Wills tipped his hat to them.

John and I had to go to work, but Earline didn't want to leave, so John just said, "Shoot, honey, stay and enjoy yourself. Somebody's bound to take you home." Now that was an understatement. Earline was so good-looking you couldn't stand it. John shouldn't have encouraged her. Maybe she would've done the same thing anyway, in fact I'm sure she would've. You know what I mean. I don't need to go into the details, except to say it was the last time we would see Earline for a while. Finally she came dragging in and John took her back. He was no paragon of virtue himself. He'd done the same thing himself more than a time or two.

As the years passed, things fell apart.

John ended up in prison and he died there.

Earline went back to Evening Shade.

Bob Wills got old and sick, and after a stroke was confined to a wheelchair. A few years ago, just before his death in the spring of 1975, J. B. Walling threw a tribute for Wills one Monday night in Fort Worth at the Tarrant County Convention Center. It was a big to-do, and Earline came down and we went to see it. It was wonderful, in a way, seeing the old Playboys and all the stars of country music. Roy Acuff, Tex Ritter, Merle Haggard and many others were there. The actor, Chill Wills, came, and so did the governor, Preston Smith.

But when Bob Wills was rolled out in his wheelchair, when he tried to talk and sing, "Take it, Leon," when he tried to yodel the way he used to, it just didn't work. He was practically a dead man. It was pathetic, and Earline cried. "Take me home, Billy," she sniffled. "I can't bear to watch anymore. Bless his poor heart."

* * *

Way Out West

Any road you take from Fort Worth to Lubbock is a long mother, so Nanette and I decided to take our time in the old Buick and get off the interstate and see what we could see. Spring had come. It might be pleasant. Funny I use the maternal in describing the road West. It was, and is, male, no matter how you go.

We angled out of Fort Worth north of Interstate 20 and followed the Brazos through places like Graham, Seymour, Guthrie and Dickens. And what we saw was a monotony of plains interrupted now and then by towns as drab and functional as loading pens and farm-to-market shipping points. After a while, the fact that you go from plains rolling and rocky to plains high and flat, that you move from the domain of the rancher to that of the farmer, makes little difference. It is all so leveling. Somehow the big sky, the long views, the exchange between prairie and plain, basin and range, are not dramatic enough to hearten the traveler in his creep across, as one native put it, the face of boredom.

And yet the names they have given their places suggest anything but ennui. Something has happened between the founding and the realization, the planting and the harvest. If drab, work-a-day, utilitarian, masculine towns called Idalou, Kitalou, Oriana, Grace and Vera have women, they have forgotten the lilt of their names and natures and have their women the way deserts have them, not as sirens in oases, but as hard-handed, hardheaded housekeepers and cooks and brood mamas. The land and the elements are so rough and primal in West Texas that the women, the women you hear about but rarely see, have all but shut themselves inside, since it is futile to try to plant grass and flowers or do anything to bring grace to that bitter and unyielding land. As far as I can tell, the few rural West Texas women who actually exist don't sin or honky-tonk. A cowboy on the 6666 Ranch in Guthrie has to drive a hundred miles and more to relieve his loneliness on a Saturday night. The country music radio reaches far and wide, but whiskey is as hard to come by as women and fancy, especially in the part above Odessa, Midland and San Angelo.

And yet the land is, to the rancher and the farmer, a paradox, even in its contrariness. For it has proven to be a bountiful and giving region, if not a Paradise, long as a striving man has a friend in the banker and plenty of room and enough water to make up for the routine denials wrought by Mother Nature, local Baptists and the federal government. Great fortunes have been made out here, not only in oil and gas but in beef and cotton and grain. Also great misfortunes. But it must be that promise that keeps towheaded kids coming out of the Future Farmers of America chapters in settlements like Spur, rearing to take on the Great Plains and bring it to its knees. The weathered old domino players can't tell the young otherwise, for they themselves remain, going through the motion of giving battle and matching wits even as they wither.

It came up a hard, windshield-cracking hail of a rain about halfway to Lubbock, somewhere out around Goree. It blew so hard my wipers froze, as if in surrender. Then, around Crosbyton, the storm stopped and the sun came out. Beautiful, we thought. It's a breeze the rest of the way. I rolled down windows and enjoyed the rise across the red caprock and the leveling out onto the High Plains. Nothing but miles and miles of furrowed farmland running away to the horizon. Lord, the crop money that must go into those unending fields. Not a tree in sight.

"What ever happened to flora and fauna?" I said.

"They moved back to Nacogdoches years ago," Nanette quipped.

Suddenly, the sky darkened in the West. More rain, I thought. But no, as we drew closer, it reddened. The sky was not raining rain but dust. The wind coming down out of the mountains of New Mexico had lifted up millions of tons of topsoil, and, like some cosmic landscaper, was redistributing it across West Texas. This was worse than the rain I had left behind. No window or seam in the old Buick was tight enough to keep out the grit, and we began to sneeze and try to breathe through handkerchiefs. It got so reddishly dark I had to stop on the shoulder and wait for the storm to pass. At last it went on, but there was still a pall of dust for a hundred miles, and later, on the outskirts of Lubbock, when it rained again the air was so full of dust that Nanette said it had not rained but mudded.

We could not leave Lorenzo without stopping at a gas station and cleaning the air filter over the carburetor. The fellow who helped me said he was going to tell his old lady not to bother cooking supper.

"Ever'thang'll be grit anyway," he said. "I'll just tell her we'll have sweet milk and the cornbread left over from last night. I don't thank the dust's gotten into the icebox. But you never can tell."

Lubbock

Preston Smith's old stomping ground. Lubbock of the prairie fires and sandstorms. Lubbock of the tornadoes and tumbleweeds. Look Out! Here come the Red Raiders and the John Birchers. As Neal R. Peirce wrote in his book, *The Great Plains States of America*, the people of the plains tend to be tough, independent, politically conservative types — "in some people's eyes, the purest examples of *Tejano erectus* to be found anywhere." But beneath the hard mask are some swingers. After all, the town's most famous native sons are not known for their sobriety. They include Bobby Layne, Buddy Holly, Mac Davis, John Denver and Joe Ely. Surely, they must have swung a few gals out at the old Cotton Club, which is still my choice. But there are some new places which are popular.

RED RAIDER CLUB
6024 Ave. A
Lubbock

Originally the Red Raider Club and Motel (which is adjacent) were bought by former Texas Tech player Donny Anderson. Club manager Sandra Patterson says she thinks the dancehall part used to be a banquet hall. Anyway,

Bob Myer has owned the place for the last few years. A new club called Coldwater might be the nearest rival to the Red Raider, but the R.R. has been there longer, and continues to bring in name entertainment. The house band is Larry Johnson. Coldwater Country keeps the place from being overrun by college kids, so the crowd is a pretty good mix. Open seven days, with entertainment Tuesday through Saturday. Cover on Friday, Saturday and Sunday.

COLDWATER COUNTRY
7301 University
Lubbock

Coldwater Country used to be called the Coldwater Cattle Company. That is, until one day when a rancher drove up in front of the place with a load of cattle to make a delivery. See, he got the honky-tonk in Lubbock mixed up with the Coldwater Cattle Company in Amarillo. Which is — of all things — a *cattle company*. Well, the folks in Amarillo didn't take too kindly to the name-filching, so the owners of the honky-tonk changed the name.

It's easy to see how the mistake could be made. Coldwater Country just looks like an old warehouse from the outside. And inside they've got metal folding chairs. Not exactly posh. They do have a game room and the biggest dancefloor in West Texas, which is a tip-off right there that this is no place for a cattle auction. Maybe a cattle call, though. Lots of Tech kids come to Coldwater to dance to different bands every week as do folks from the surrounding farms. The headliner is the Maines Brothers, who signed with Mercury Records recently. Merle Haggard played the grand opening a few years back, and stars like Conway Twitty make appearances at Coldwater. They're open Wednesday through Saturday, 8 till 2.

JUG LITTLE'S COTTON CLUB
Slaton Highway
Lubbock

Times have changed since Ralph Lowe built the Cotton Club in the '40s. And so have the liquor zones in Lubbock. Jug Little hosts only 10 public dances a year at his Cotton Club (he's owned it the last four years) because he's outside of the Lubbock city limits in dry Precinct No. 2. Jug can't make enough money on a *byob* basis to stay open all the time and compete with clubs in Lubbock that can serve liquor by the drink. However, if you miss one of the public dances (they're usually on holidays and such), Jug'll host your private party just as sure as you're looking at him. He can seat 965 (can you be a little more specific, Jug?), has a big bar and a wooden dancefloor.

Once you could go to the Cotton Club to hear Buddy Holly or Elvis. Now Jug hires locals, but the old Cotton Club still has a certain feel about it. So if you're heading into Lubbock on the Slaton Hwy. from Post, look on your left for a white building with brown trim, and hope it's a holiday and time for a shindig.

* * *

More Car Trouble

We were going to come back east through Post and try the Red Rooster, where I had danced twenty years before, and then slide down through Snyder and Sweetwater to Abilene. But we hadn't gotten out of Lubbock before the fan came off the engine of the old Buick and clattered around under the hood.

"What now?" Nanette said. What she meant was that I should have listened to her and left the Buick in the barn.

"Call Lopez," I said.

"How can he help us in Kaufman? That's 400 miles away!"

"I don't mean that Lopez. I mean the one here."

"You know a mechanic named Lopez in Lubbock?"

"No," I said, "but I know there is one here."

"How do you know that?"

"Experience, child. There's a mechanic named Lopez in every town in Texas, and he's always as cheap and honest as a mechanic can be, which puts him just below itinerant roofers and a cut above doctors, lawyers and bankers."

Nanette put her hands on her pretty little high hips. "Well," she said, skeptically, "where will we find this Lopez? In the Yellow Pages?"

"Nothing so swell as that," I had to admit. "We'll go door to door in Mexican town . . ."

"You will," she said. "I'm walking back to the motel."

I found Lopez in a garage behind his house on Idalou Road.

"Can you put a fan in a 1955 Buick."

"Si, you got the fan I can."

"It's broken. One of the blades is half in two."

"You got the other half?"

"No, it must have fallen through the engine to the ground."

"Well, let's look at her anyhow."

He drove me back to my 1955 Buick in his 1983 Buick.

"I'll call one of my sons with the wrecker," he said. "I can fix that mother. I can cut a piece of tin and weld it to the broken blade, and that ought to hold you till you get home and order a new one."

And that's what he did. While I waited I phoned Paul at Wisniewski and asked him to send me a fan to the bus station in Abilene, where I'd pick it up in a couple of days.

On the way, just sightseeing, we dropped down into Lynn County and Tahoka, and I was reminded of some talk I heard back in 1978 when I was at a Tahoka social function.

"I really would like to see a good hard rain and a wet oil well," Callaway Huffacre said. He spotted an old friend and embraced her. "Honey," he said, "I'm still countin' on marrying you, but Grandma won't give me a divorce. She thinks I'm too sweet."

"Oh, Callaway, you're a mess. But you are sweet."

Buel Draper, who had just driven in from his farm, was telling Police Chief Jack Miller about how Pearl Brewing in San Antonio was putting out a new label called Billy Beer, after the president's brother. "I've got some in my car," Buel said, "but I'm afraid to open it. I'm afraid it might pop and piss all over me."

C. Newton Starnes saw me raise my eyebrow. "Don't get the wrong idea," he said. "Tahoka is a clean town." Starnes was the Methodist preacher.

"Yeah," Buel shot back, "swept clean by the wind and dirt."

"Well," the preacher admitted, eyeing Buel, "We do have a ringtail tooter or two."

Abilene

In the beginning, Abilene looked as if it might be another rip-roaring railroad town, but the pious tightened the buckle of the Bible Belt on it so tight that for almost a hundred years the closest things to a dance out here were the spirals and jigs of the dust devils on the sandy flats. Now that the town's wet you can have a good time if you don't overdo it. If there's one thing the people hate, it's intemperance. So the bouncers are big and the drinks are watered. But the music's 108 proof. And Lopez of Abilene is a good mechanic. He installed the fan I'd gotten from Wisniewski with no problem.

PONDEROSA BALLROOM
3881 Vine
Abilene

L.C. Agnew had been a C&W bandleader for thirty-seven years before he opened the Ponderosa Ballroom, where he and the Dixie Playboys play every night. L.C. holds that the Playboys are probably the oldest continuous country band in Texas, started by his uncle in Cisco, Texas back in 1929. The Ponderosa is a modern place — carpet and all — with a "strictly mixed" crowd, but the atmosphere is old fashioned. "No drunks, no hats on the dancefloor, no loud cussin'," says L.C. You may fit in with the "young, old, and some ugly" customers. Hours are 3:30 p.m. to midnight Monday through Friday, 3:30 till 1 a.m. Saturday and a matinee performance Sunday at 4.

Midland-Odessa

Twin cities of the Great Plains, they sit 20 miles apart on the Permian Basin, that fount of grassland, potash, oil and gas, which makes the area headquarters not only for farming and ranching but the largest inland petrochemical complex in the United States. Some say that there is a distinct difference in the cities, that Midland is where white-collar executives sit in skyscrapers and count their millions while Odessa is a hard-hat town where the dirty work that goes to make those millions is done. The oil action has slowed down, but these are still boom towns that continue to sprawl across the plain. Like everything else, the honky-tonks have gone uptown. Many of the old dance halls like the Tumbleweed Club in Odessa have withered on the vine, and the newer places, such as Graham Central Station in Odessa, mix country and western with rock 'n roll and pop. We did find two new but true blue C&W places.

STARDUST
1006 S. Midkiff
Midland

Manager Donny Henderson says the Stardust is the only honky-tonk in Midland, and you have to go to the Stardust in Odessa if you don't like it. They're both owned by Herbert Graham, who owns several clubs in the area. Stardust (Midland) is a pretty modern-looking place. They've got a big dancefloor ("The biggest in Midland," says Henderson) and serve mixed drinks. The crowd varies, but they're between 19 and 55, most of the time. Pepper Martin and the Pepper Martin Band plays Tuesday through Sunday. The club is open six days from 7 p.m. until 2 a.m. It's a Spanish stucco facade that has been there for five years. Parts of *Waltz Across Texas* were filmed at Stardust. Everyone is real proud Pepper Martin has started to cut records.

CHAPTER 10

The Panhandle

Driving north, we climbed up into the Staked Plains, the Llano Estacado, one of the most perfect plains regions in the world. It covers most of the Texas Panhandle, 70,000 square miles, and can be described as a giant, irregular-shaped mesa, a massive table top that pokes up from the flats at heights from three hundred to a thousand feet. Llano means plain, estacado means staked, thus staked plain. But why? The Comancheros, Mexicans who traded with the Comanches, tell us that's what the Indians called it, because it was the plain where it was necessary to stake their horses, else a tumbleweed would frighten them and they would run forever.

Amarillo

Droughts, financial panics and grasshopper plagues. That's the bad, that and the taste of the water. Cattle, cotton, wheat, oil and gas. That's the good. Queen of the Panhandle, a proud, yellow-painted lady of the prairie. Out on the road to Buffalo Springs a duded-up old prospector named Dusty Miller welcomed us to the Big Texan Steak Ranch, where saloon Sallies in garters served up pan-fried steak. But don't let this good time regalia fool you. Amarillo, even in its prosperity, is a rather high-minded and severe city, essentially conservative, and has as much culture with at least a middle C as it has honky-tonks. Even in the dance halls the riff-raff are not all that welcome. But the Panhandle counties are dry save for a wet spot here and there, and the wettest precincts and the only honky-tonks are in Amarillo, which, in its loyalty to its high plains isolation, is one of the more interesting cities in Texas.

The oldest honky-tonks in Amarillo are the Avalon Ballroom and the Aviatrix Club, and there's still life in them on weekends. But it is the newer dance halls which draw the young and the money. Amarillo may have a symphony orchestra and a ballet, but C&W is still its favorite music. Even the Hilton Inn at the airport has a club called the Butterfield Junction which features live country music every night and dancing on a stainless steel floor.

CARAVAN EAST
3601 Olsen Blvd.
Amarillo

The Caravan East sports the largest sign in Amarillo — 60 feet high, 20 feet long with 488 lights rimming the edges alone. In all there are about 1,000 lights on the sign, which is definitely Las Vegas style. So is the honky-tonk. Manager Richard Smith explains: "The Caravan caters completely to the adult crowd. We may also be unique in that we are the only nightclubs (there are six Caravan Easts in Texas and New Mexico) where you have to check your hat at the door. You can wear nice Levi's, but no plain white t-shirts. The way we see it, a true Texas gentleman won't have any problem leaving his hat at the door. When there was the urban cowboy movement, we had some problems, but not anymore. A true Texas gentleman never gives a beef about it. See, in the late 1800's, the bars started making cowboys check their guns at the door. It cut down on the fighting. So does checking your hat. It takes away from the macho-ness."

Caravan East is big — 12,000 square feet. It's carpeted and even has chandeliers. The only place in Amarillo that even comes close to being as pretty as the Caravan East is Champs, and it's rock 'n' roll. Caravan seats 600 and employs B.W. Davis and the Quicksilver Band as the house entertainment. They rotate road bands and occasionally bring in stars like the Bellamy Brothers, Brenda Lee and Louise Mandrell. They are open seven days a week, and feature two bands nightly, rotating regular road bands. Get there early, as Smith said, "It's always packed by 5, and there ain't nowhere to sit."

RODEO
2700 S. Georgia
Amarillo

At times a little risque with its special attractions — i.e., the Wednesday lingerie show called Intimate Expression — Rodeo is not the kind of dance hall my friend Bill K. Forbus would frequent (ahem, least not with Patsy), but it seems to serve a need on Amarillo's south side. Open only a year, it draws a crowd of honky-tonkers who like their music tight and fast. Manager Marshall Wood has just hired away Tom Meyers' Country Pride from the Caravan as house band. Clyde Logg, one of the best country bands in the Panhandle, plays regularly at Rodeo. Wood books acts off the circuit like Alvin Crow and Whiskey River. A trio of Amarillo dudes — Chip Dunn, Steve Howell and Neil Scott — own Rodeo, and they've given manager Wood a free and fanciful hand. "We like to have fun here at Rodeo," Wood says, "and since sex sells, we encourage the girls to come out, because right behind them will be the boys. The more off the wall, the better we like it." You can't miss the place. It's a big, red brick building with old barn wood touches and a lot of cactus and yucca out front beneath the neon sign. Open seven days a week, house band live from 5:15 p.m. to 8:30, then the featured band takes over and goes till 2 a.m. Mixed drinks, beer and wine.

AVALON BALLROOM II
2624 Amarillo Blvd. East
Amarillo

Don't get the wrong impression from that Roman numeral II. Avalon isn't some new faddish C&W chain with sister club I and sister club III scattered shrewdly about to rake in the customers. The original Avalon Ballroom burned to the ground 11 years ago, and they resurrected it on the spot as quick as they could and went on with the dancing. So the old green brick hall and its era is called I and the new green brick hall is II. The owners and managers have come and gone. Bill Aikens had it when Honest Jess ran the joint, and then Homer Meils bought it. Tim Morrison is now the owner and J.L. Edwards the manager. And yes, there were others before them. The Avalon is so old its age is misty with legend. One constant is that its customers are loyal. They've been dancing at the ballroom so long folks in the Panhandle call it the "Smooth-Mouth Club." A longtime regular swears that there isn't a set of real teeth in the house. Billie Freeman says that's bull. Billie, bless her heart, is the other constant at the Avalon. She's been a waitress there since Harry S. Truman was president and she says her teeth are her own, thank you. She's full of stories and Billie says the worst day that ever befell the Avalon was not the fire but the time the precinct voted in liquor by the drink. "Mixed drinks ruined it for the old crowd," she recalls. "They couldn't afford to pay the cover and drink $2 drinks all night. Now we're back to beer again and our regulars have come back. We'll serve set-ups for those who bring their own bottle, but here we're mostly beer drinkers." The Avalon is open Friday and Saturday from 7 p.m. until 2 a.m. Live bands like Shiloh and Tiny Duncan rotate during the two nights.

* * *

The Dancing Dentist From Dumas

I'm the Ding Dong Daddy from Dumas
And you oughta see me do my strut.

Just a rinka dinka daddy from Dumas
Oh, you oughta see me do my stuff.

I'm a peach-fry papa from Jackson
    Hollow
And you oughta see me do my strut.

I'm a honey-drippin' daddy,
Got a hard-hatted baby —
She's a sheik-shaking Sheba —
And hallelujah!

I'm a ding dong daddy from Dumas
And you oughta see me do my stuff.
"I'm a Ding Dong Daddy From Dumas"
by Phil Baxter

Bill and Patsy Forbus are the kind of people, who, when they're visiting their grown kids in Dallas, will spend all day splashing at White Water or seeing the sights and riding the rides at Six Flags. Get the picture? I've been in Dallas 14 years and have never, not for one second, considered going to such places. You couldn't get me there with a team of mules. The Forbuses drive from Dumas to Dallas — a distance of 417 miles — to have clean family fun. The saltiest thing I've ever heard Bill say is "Gee, Gosh." Patsy is a school teacher and her father was a dentist. Bill is a dentist. And he and Patsy are happy that their daughter married a dentist and that their son is a Dallas banker. On top of that, they are high school sweethearts, church-going teetotalers and probably (maybe only conservative enough to be) Republicans. Bill is so solidly bourgeoisie that he's very big in the Texas Dental Association, will probably soon become its president. For seven years he's been chairman of the TDA's state political action committee and is going on to greater influence as a national PAC committeeman. If all this respectability was behind anyone else but Bill Forbus, I'd get up and leave the room when I saw him coming. Life is too short to waste on boring Babbitts. But in Bill's case *I'm* not making an exception. *He is* the exception. He's the Ding Dong Daddy from Dumas. That makes the rest of it all right, because friend, when day is done and night is nigh, when the honky-tonk opens and the band takes the stand, the first feet to hit the floor at the first note are Bill's and Patsy's. They are the dancingest couple I've seen in all my years of high times in Texas. We don't have dance marathons anymore, but if one ever comes up, I'm entering the Forbuses and laying Harvey Fodell's money on them. Harvey is my father-in-law but he won't mind. He's watched Bill and Patsy dance since their dental student days at Baylor Med, and he says Saint Vitus can't touch them. Yeah, I know. Harvey is a dentist, too. But he has *his* surprising side as well. They have to have something. Think what they face every day.

At night Bill Forbus steps out of the white coat of Dr. Jekyll and dons his Mr. Hyde, and away he and the fetching, yellow-haired Patsy go, dancing. Every time I saw them in Dallas they wanted to go country and western kicking, and it ended up with the rest of us sitting on the sidelines at Belle Starr catching our breaths and wondering when Bill and Patsy were going to tire out. Bill is not much taller than Harvey and me, but he's in better shape if stamina is any indication. I watched him one night and, out of envy, kept hoping his toupee would fall off.

"He must have that rug glued down with Super Bond," I observed, winking at Harvey.

Harvey gave me a funny look. "Rug? You talking about Bill?"

"Yeah. Isn't that a wig he's wearing. I've never seen such perfect, sculpted hair."

Harvey slid off his chair and rolled around on the floor in the sawdust and cigarette butts. "Oh, my God! Oh, my God! That's a scream."

Kathy is Harvey's beautiful blonde wife. She is prettier than June Haver used to be. She drives a Mercedes 450 SL and looks as young as her daughters. Even though I'm old enough to be her big brother I like to call her "Mother" like Nanette and Cindy do. "Mother," I said, "what's wrong with Harvey?"

"Oh," she said brightly. "Is he on the floor again? Harvey honey, what are you doing down there?"

"I'm dying," he said. "Billy thinks Bill Forbus wears a toupee."

Kathy looked at me sweetly and laughed. "No son," she said. "He's always had a beautiful, thick head of hair. He isn't bald like you."

Sweet family. Really a sweet family I married into.

* * *

It made sense, of course, that when Nanette and I set out for the Panhandle we used Bill and Patsy as our guides to the best honky-tonks. Typically, they were thorough about it because they had spent years testing every amusement hall within driving distance of Dumas, which is halfway between Amarillo and the Oklahoma border on a north/south line, and just about halfway between the New Mexican and Oklahoma border on a west/east line. The distances are great out here, and the towns are few and far between, but we found that Panhandlers think nothing about driving from here to hell and gone for a good time. The wildest story I heard was about the couple in Dalhart who were hungry for seafood. They got up at the crack of dawn on a Saturday, drove down through the Panhandle, across North Texas, on down to Houston and out to Galveston Island, arriving at Gaido's in time for a late supper. He had a seaman's platter and beer. She had lobster and wine. He thought it was worth it, she said the lobster was a little tough. They got in their car and drove during the night all the way back home, getting there in time to make the noon services at church. By Wednesday of the next week she was complaining he never took her out. Patsy can never make that charge against Bill. He takes her dancing two nights a week.

But I must warn you that going dancing with the Forbuses is not like going dancing with George Jones and Tammy Wynette. Bill and Patsy usually pass on Saturday nights. They don't like to mess with the drunks on the highway and in the clubs. Besides, they get up early on Sunday for church. Wednesday is their for-sure dancing night. Here's the way it usually goes:

Bill shuts people's mouths about two in the afternoon, closes the office and drives home. Patsy is still at school. He showers and shaves, puts on Levis, a short-sleeve plaid shirt, pulls on his boots and taps his fingers and practices his moves until Patsy gets home just before four. She jumps in the shower, comes out in jeans or a denim skirt, and they hit U.S. 287 for Amarillo.

Forty-eight miles and forty-eight minutes later they pull up to the Caravan on Olsen Boulevard. It is still daylight. Just about five, when B.W. Davis and his Quicksilver Band start the live music. Often, during that first hour, Bill and Patsy are the only couple on the floor. Surely they're the only ones drinking Cokes. They dance every tune Quicksilver plays, and when the band takes a break Bill and Patsy dance to the jukebox. They only pause to gulp a Coke and go to the john. They continue in this manner until around seven, when some of their friends start coming in and they loosen up and trade partners and visit with one another. There's Dr. Lee Cranfill and his wife, Gay, also from Dumas. An Amarillo fireman, Joe Jackson and his wife, R.M.

Every honky-tonk has a character, and the favorite at the Caravan is 86-year-old Frank Bezner, a retired farmer who drives in from his place at Hereford, 46 miles away, to dance several times a week. "He is always here when we are," Bill said. "Now there's a guy with a toupee, that and a cigar, those are his trademarks. He dances with every woman in the place and he's a gentleman about it. We all love him."

And then there is the mysterious couple from out of town. Tall, elegant, beautifully matched in physique and grace, they wear matching outfits which vary from week to week. As they glide around the dance floor they kiss. "They don't just kiss now and then," Bill observed. "They kiss and smooch constantly while dancing like a million bucks!" The rumor going 'round is that while they are meant for each other they are married to others, and the Caravan is their rendezvous.

No matter how much fun they are having, Bill and Patsy stop dancing at eight, after three hours, and mosey over to the free sandwich bar and have supper. The Caravan doesn't stint. There's even barbecue on the house, and since Bill and Patsy have been drinking Cokes two-for-one on the happy hour, their total bill for the evening comes to $2.90. "It always comes to that," Bill said. "Wonderful. Worth the drive."

Now they pull their Cinderella act and exit. It's not even nine o'clock.

But they don't take the highway home. Not directly. First they go by Zack's and order two big cups of frozen yogurt — "And it only costs $2.29 for two!" — which they slurp on the drive back to Dumas.

There are, as we mention in the roundup, other places to honky-tonk in the Panhandle, and Bill and Patsy have been to them all. But the Caravan suits them best because they can get in early to live music and get out before the crowd takes over. And then there's two-for-ones and free eats. George Jones may be a drunk and a wastrel, but not Bill K. Forbus.

He and Patsy are not just country-western dancers. They rock and they roll, they jitterbug, and as ballroom dancers they have a Latin flair for the rumba, the samba and the cha-cha-cha. For these refinements they repair to the Amarillo Club on the top floor of the American National Bank.

The Forbuses always loved to dance, but they did not get into it with such regular rhapsody until after Patsy recovered from a serious illness. Her ordeal gave pause to Bill. He had been pulling teeth hammer and tong, going at his profession with the intensity of a country boy bent on making something of himself, and then, all of a sudden he was faced with the chance that he might lose the most important person in his life. It turned him around. He had already lost Ollie Forbus, the woman who had plucked him from a Tulsa orphanage, and he had lost his sis who had taught him to dance. Bill began to sort out for himself the things that were most important to him, and profession and money took a backseat to Patsy and the family. The girl he had loved since Hereford High became the women he would celebrate for the rest of his days. Patsy returns the love. That's how they live. It is beautiful.

CHAPTER 11

The Trans-Pecos

This is no place to honky-tonk. The Mexicans call it El Despoblado, the uninhabited, the empty place. It is rough desert country, basin and range, range and basin, and covers an area the size of Florida. Johnnie Chambers, the rancher's wife who teaches in the one-room school at Candelaria on the Rio Grande, had just finished counting heads in the 25 Trans-Pecos counties for the U.S. Census, and she said there were roughly 59,000 people in the 59,000-square miles between Langtry and El Paso and between the Rio Grande and the Pecos. Most of them are stove up in the little towns and settlements you come across now and then. "We've also determined," Mrs. Chambers said, "that there are only four white women between the Rimrock and the river and between Presidio and Jeff Davis County."

"Who are they?"

"The Howard sisters who run the store here at Candelaria; Carolyn Moorhead, who with her husband runs the camp down at Ruidosa Hot Springs; and yours truly."

"Do any of you honky-tonk?"

She laughed. "The Howard sisters wouldn't. Carolyn and her husband might, even though he's a preacher he'll take a snort. I dang sure would if Boyd was in a good mood and we had the time it took to drive from here to, say, Puny's in Pecos, or on into El Paso. But shoot, Billy, we're talking about 200 miles in each direction, two hundred going and two hundred returning. It'd make more sense to stay at home, crack a beer and turn up the radio."

What Johnnie Chambers said is true. Even north of the Pecos at Monahans we found the doors of the old Green Lantern and West End Clubs closed. Puny's was open in Pecos itself, but they weren't at all friendly, and when I started asking questions the bartender made me to understand that the kind of place they ran there was none of my business. It has been around since Genesis, and obviously serves a purpose for those parched souls out there, but not for strangers. Found no honky-tonks in any of the towns out in the great middle of El Despoblado. Nothing at Van Horn, Ft. Davis, Ft. Stockton, Marfa, Alpine, Sanderson and Ozona.

Langtry, home of the bewhiskeyed old judge, turned out to be an oasis of sorts. If you're tired of work, tired of your mate, tired of watching the Border Patrol wait for wetbacks, tired of watching the tourists come and go to Judge Bean's Jersey Lilly Saloon, which hasn't served San Antonio lager beer since 1903, about the only thing you can do is drop in at Bud and Pansy's Cafe, the nearest watering hole for 60 miles. The Dyers offer a God-send. Their barbecue is spicy, their beer is cold, and Marty Robbins and Chubby Wise are on the jukebox. You can slide the tables apart to dance and there's even a pool table.

El Paso

As we entered El Paso, the passage to the North for early Spanish explorers, we came across mile after mile of real estate development signs, promising Edens in the arid hills for a little down and a little each month. Closer into town, Cinema Park, a three-screen drive-in theater set in the middle of tract housing, featured "Zula Dawn," "Naked Stew Girl," "Cheaper To Keep Her," and "Mother's Day." El Paso will run out of water and dry up someday if they are not successful in suing New Mexico for water, but never mind. Down the road from the outdoor dirty movies was one of the city's newest attractions, a water slide. Alongside the road, in the ditches, trash and litter had replaced tumbleweeds. Ah, what has happened to old El Paso? It's old Mexican grace has been buried under miles and miles of asphalt and franchise road houses. We passed through many a bar and cantina before we finally found a real, live C&W place. Doing the tour I was reminded of Dolph Briscoe's quest for votes in El Paso during the spring primary of 1978. At the Tigua Indian Reservation Dolph and Janey watched aboriginal Americans perform the friendship dance. The governor's face fell when the Indians asked him to join them in the circle. Dolph balked, turned red in the face and looked to Janey for help.

Off to one side, the governor's old friend, Judge Woodrow Wilson Bean, snickered. "Hell," he said, "the son-of-a bitch is so self-conscious he can't even waltz."

But Janey made him do it. The governor got up, and though greatly embarrassed, danced with the Indians.

Judge Bean roared. "I can't believe it! He's going to do it. Oh, it's a shame what a man has to go through for public office." The judge cupped his hands and hollered at the governor, "Dolph, don't do it. The race isn't that close. There's not twenty votes in the whole tribe!"

The judge turned out to be right, but not in the way he thought. Briscoe ran behind John Hill, who lost to Bill Clements in the general election.

After all those miles and a week's time, we can, with conscience, recommend only one honky-tonk in the whole damned Trans-Pecos.

CARAVAN EAST
8759 Gateway East
El Paso

This is another of the four Caravan East clubs in the Southwest. (Others in Amarillo, Pueblo, N.M., and Albuquerque). A pretty fancy showplace where you'll probably feel out of it in jeans. Truckers along I-30, which fronts the club, have been known to wash and shower and change clothes at nearby truck stops so they can have a night at Caravan East. Gentlemen check your hats at the door. The cover may stab you. It's $7 apiece, but chandeliers will light your way as you dance to two bands a night, seven nights a week. And they book the best C&W stars. Swanky digs, but comfortable, and there's a free sandwich bar if you dance up a hunger.

CHAPTER 12

Mexican Texas

> If you're ever down in Texas
>   and feeling all alone
> There's a lot of kicker places
>   just south of San Antone.
> Ain't nothing fancy mind ya'
>   just a place where good folks go
> You can hear the boot heels
>   start to click
> When they play the Cotton-Eyed Joe.
>
> *Texas Fiddle Song*
> *by Leona Williams and Rob Williams*
> *sung by Merle Haggard*

Leona and Rob knew what they were writing about. Folks in the southern tail of Texas take a backseat to nobody when it comes to honky-tonking. The only Texans who come close to keeping step with the kickers from south of San Antone are those from the hill country and maybe the big cities of Dallas, Fort Worth and Houston. That lower Texas should be blessed with dance halls ought not surprise anyone, since it is the home of the Mexican, perhaps the most musical of American folk. But a Mexican cantina, no matter how loud the ranchero music and how passionate the polkas, is not a honky-tonk. It is the honky-tonk's equivalent among its people, but there the similarity ends. A honky-tonk is for poor white folks and reflects our culture, or at least it did until recently. Since there are more poor Mexicans than anything else in South Texas, how is it that there are so many honky-tonks? The answer is that the second-most numerous people in Mexican Texas are rednecks. They are the farmboys and cowpokes and oil field roughnecks and such, and they have joined with the Mexicans and the Germans to keep the arid half of the state as wet and as cheerful as possible under often droughty conditions.

Remember the dry-wet line that splits Texas north and south, prohibitionist and pub-crawler? Drive eighty miles below that despicable demarcation to the northern border of Reeves County on the Pecos and then slide down east-southeast on a pepper string to the coast and the northern boundary of Calhoun County, and you have the *Tortilla Curtain,* a rough parallel to the temperance belt. Drive south from any point along the curtain and note how the concentration of Texans who speak Spanish thickens. The road signs symbolize the change as much as the cactus and mesquite and the ranchero music on the car radio. The stop signs bear a second word, *Alto.* In the fifty southern counties the population is more than 50 percent *Tejano* (Spanish for Texan), and in the seventeen counties along the Mexican border it is as high as 85 percent *Tejano.*

But, as I say, don't let this discourage you in your search for honky-tonks. The whites of Mexican Texas — that is, the Anglo-Celts and the Germans — are so dead-set in their ethnocentric ways that they have fiercely guarded the sanctity of their dancing and drinking houses. Now it's true that some of the Irish have married into Mexican families, but that was politics and business, the blending of the old, land-grant rich with the new, land-hungry hustlers. When it comes to empire, even race takes a breather to the expedient. But generally out here in Cactusland there is a clear distinction between them that drink mescal and shuffle to the Fat Mexican Polka and them that quaff malt and sour mash and hop to the schottische and Cotton-Eyed Joe. The gringos are more profane and earthy, especially the young in the looser joints. They've turned the old breakdown, "Cotton-Eyed Joe," which Bob Wills resurrected and made popular in the 1940's, into a shitkicker's hoot which is danced and shouted all over the state now.

It's a line dance with kicks and promenade and a running dialogue between the caller (either the lead singer or the fiddler) and the dancers. The caller can say anything he wants, but the dancers' reply is set. It is always "BULL-SHIT!" and shouted in unison. It might go like this:

Caller: STEPPED IN WHAT?
Dancers: BULL-SHIT!
Caller: WHAT 'CHU SAY?
Dancers: BULL-SHIT!
Caller: SAY YOU'RE A STUD?
Dancers: BULL-SHIT!
Caller: AND THE LADY'S A VIRGIN?
Dancers: BULL-SHIT!
Caller: BOSS SAYS DRINKS ON THE HOUSE!

Dancers: BULL-SHIT!
Caller: PREZADENT SAYS GOOD TIMES A'COMIN'!
Dancers: BULL-SHIT!
Caller: WHAT 'CHU SAY?
Dancers: BULL-SHIT!

A Mexican Standoff

You might have noticed J.A.'s place, or rather his wife's place, if you were ever on U.S. 81 between Austin and San Antonio. Perhaps you missed it. It is rather small. If you are going toward San Antonio, they are on the right, this side of Selma, the white frame building with the neon sign and the gravel driveway, home of The Crystal Ball Nite Club and Dance Hall, home of J.A. and Lupe, who sleep in a room in the back.

J.A. describes himself as an Anglo gentleman of inept middle age. Lupe is a faded Mexican flower of debatable age who pops Dentyne, bosses J.A. and tries to hustle some business on that stretch of highway. It is difficult. All they have is warm beer and a jukebox and a revolving, fake crystal ball which Lupe thinks is lovely when lit but which offends J.A. It has Pearl Beer advertised on it, and although J.A. thinks Pearl is a good beer, he thinks it shouldn't be emblazoned on their crystal ball. It is a matter of taste, he points out. Lupe says he shouldn't complain. They got the ball free from the route man.

They get by. When J.A. thinks about it, he can't imagine why Lupe married him, unless she was flattered by a gringo offering honorable intentions. She has had her share of hard knocks and had come to expect the worst. J.A. guesses he surprised her. And he's sure he impressed her that evening in San Antonio when then Governor Preston Smith walked up to their table in the Pan American Cafe and stuck out his hand and said, "J.A., you old sonofagun, long time no see!" They were married right after that.

J.A. suspects that Lupe even thought he would lend a little class to the club, but he says of course he hasn't. He says he is too gray and rumpled and childish. He lacks the vitality of the truckers who drink there. The back of his head is vulnerable with a bald spot and J.A. is as small and pale as an albino mystic, a bit odd, he supposes, hating cheese and salt, never having his fill of bananas, loving words like lovely but not above saying something stronger when a fizz of beer hits him in the bifocals. I have done rougher things than you would think, J.A. says, but still he reminds himself of J. Alfred Prufrock. Oh, he is fairly well educated for a bartender, but that has served him little and certainly it is of no use there on U.S. 81 opening beer bottles for truck drivers. He measures out his life in 12 fluid oz., and because tomorrow holds nothing for him he lives in the past, not in the past of last year's visit to Six Flags, where Lupe won a chalk astronaut, but in the yellowed long ago of that first atomic bomb blast in the New Mexican desert.

J.A. was just a kid then, back in 1944 and '45, but he remembers the coming of the military and the mysterious scientists to that remote outpost of ranches near Alamogordo. His dad had been a foreman on one of the places before the government bought up everything and made an air base and bomb test site. J.A. and his family moved to another ranch many miles beyond the base, but they were always curious about what was going on out there on the old place. They heard rumors. And then of course there came the day of the detonation, July 16, 1945, when the shock wave rippled the earth for 30 miles in each direction. It was followed by a deafening roar and a mushroom cloud that could be seen for hundreds of miles away, even as far as El Paso. It scared the hell out of J.A. He had nightmares about it, still does. He has lived the years since convinced that nuclear man will destroy himself. He is a fanatic about it, to the point where he seems intent on destroying himself with booze before the bombs do it. He used to be a bore about it, buttonholing every customer with his horror story and doom-saying, but Lupe put a stop to that. Now he's not so bad about it, but the news of the leaky nuclear plant in Harrisburg, Pennsylvania, set him to brooding again and Lupe has to keep him away from the customers until his terror passes. It will. It has always come and gone in him like a bad dream. Lupe is pretty patient with him, considering her steadfast opinion that J.A.'s drinking doesn't have anything to do with the bomb. The bomb is just an excuse, she says, an excuse for J.A. to drown the devil inside him.

It isn't a bad life. He and Lupe sleep late in their little room behind the bar. J.A. can't remember when they've gotten up before noon. They hope for a good crowd on Saturday nights but then after it is over they fall into bed exhausted. A good house for them is 30 people who come in and stay till they close. Maybe that doesn't sound like many, but when there are 25 men, and 20 of them are drunk and buying for five women — if they are fortunate enough to have that many ladies — you've done a night's work just taking their money and keeping them logged with beer.

In the afternoons, Handsome Devil comes by with some hombre to prove to that hombre, with $5 on the line, that he can eat glass. And he does. He eats about a fourth of one of those cheap little beer glasses. J.A. and Lupe get the glasses free from the distributor so they don't mind, and Lupe gets as much kick out of it as Handsome Devil does in taking some hombre's money. J.A. often debates about who will kick off first, Handsome from internal bleeding or J.A. himself from internal brooding and booze. It is, at this point, a Mexican standoff.

San Antonio

The Confederate poet, Sidney Lanier, browsing about the streets of San Antonio in 1872, described it in this way: "If peculiarities were quills, San Antonio de Bexar would be a rare porcupine. Over all the round of aspects in which a thoughtful mind may view a city, it bristles with striking idiosyncrasies and bizarre contrasts . . . Here hobbles an old Mexican who looks like old Father Time in reduced circumstances, his feet, his body, his head all swathed in rags, his face a blur of wrinkles, his beard gray-grizzled — a picture of eld such as one will rarely find. There goes a little German boy who was captured a year or two ago by Indians within three miles of San Antonio, and has just been retaken and sent home a few days ago. Do you see that poor Mexican without any hands? . . . Here is a great Indian-fighter who will show you what he calls his 'vouchers,' being scraps of the red braves he has slain; there a gentleman who blew up his store here in '42 to keep the incoming Mexicans from benefiting by his goods, and who afterwards spent a weary imprisonment in that stern castle of Perote away down in Mexico, where the Mier prisoners (and who ever thinks nowadays of that strange, bloody Mier Expedition?) were confined; there, a portly, handsome, buccaneer-looking captain who led the Texans against Cortinas in '59; there a small, intelligent-looking gentleman who at twenty was first Secretary of War of the young Texan Republic, and who is said to know the history of everything that has been done in Texas from that time to this, minutely; and so on through a perfect gauntlet of people who have odd histories, odd natures or odd appearances, we reach our hotel . . ."

Much has changed but much hasn't in the last hundred and fourteen years, so tied to the past is San Antonio. The military is still there fighting imaginary wars and so are the Indians, muted in the Mexicans, and yes, they are still poor, the most of them, even if Henry Cisneros is mayor. No city in Texas has such a flavor of humanity and endless time swarming its narrow streets and beautiful winding riverwalk. Yes, there are cowboys, dance hall girls and adventurers of every stripe, plenty of thieves and politicians and faith healers. Like Lanier, we walked the streets and river, ate from chili queens and relived the siege of the Alamo with Crockett and Bowie and Travis. Nanette and I stayed at the Menger, as Lanier did, toured the Institute of Texan Cultures, stuffed ourselves at Mi Tierra Cafe in the market, and slipped a dollar to Bongo Joe (George Coleman) as he beat his big oil drums. Early in the evening we returned to the hotel to rest up and pare down for our nightly tour of the honky-tonks. Oh, and yes, Lopez of San Antonio was a super-mech. He found a water pump for the Buick that was a close enough fit, saving me another emergency call to Paul at Wisniewski. "What else can go wrong?" Nanette cried. Only a fool would have answered.

TEXAS STAR INN
7400 Bandera Rd.
San Antonio
Two miles north Loop 410

The Texas Star Inn looks kind of like the Alamo from the outside, like the Alamo *after* Santa Anna's siege. I have friends in the Leon Valley who every day for the past twenty-five years have passed the Texas Star Inn and shuddered to think what goes on there, but then they are sheltered types. The truth is that the Texas Star is as genuine a honky-tonk as is left in Texas, one that even a purist like The Professor of Honky-Tonks would stamp with legitimacy. The place has been next to that gravel pit out on the Bandera Road for forty years, which is almost but not quite as long as Dodie Sullivan and Polly Herchberger have been the hired hostesses there. Dodie and Polly have now bought out the old owners and are looking forward to forty more years of good times. They are open Tuesday through Saturday from 3 p.m. till midnight and until 2 a.m. Fridays and Saturdays. On Wednesdays, Fridays and Saturdays they have live music. Bands like Bubba Littrell, The Countrymen and Texas Gold take turns. Free dance lessons Tuesdays and Thursdays. If you're hungry, Dodie and Polly can seat 400 at brown and white checkered tablecloths upon which they serve chicken-fried steak, liver-and-onions, catfish, and burgers. This is BYOB, bub, with beer, wine and setups. The Texas Star has good character and a big dance floor. Parts of the movie, *Waltz Across Texas*, were filmed there, and though Dodie and Polly can't afford Willie Nelson anymore, they had him when he used to play bass with Ray Price's band. Dodie swears that Johnny Bush made his first nickel at Texas Star. Spend yours there and have a great night in old San Antone.

THE FARMER'S DAUGHTER
542 N.W.W. White Rd.
San Antonio

"No whistlin,' no hollerin', no midriffs, no low-cut blouses, no shirttails hangin' out, no flip-flop shoes! Damn it, we run a tight ship around here!" It may scare you off, but that's what they say keeps the Farmer's Daughter going lo these many years. Another oldie but goodie roadhouse. The place has been swinging for 22 years, and the booking contracts framed and hanging on the wall prove some of the best — George Jones, Johnny Paycheck — have played at the Farmer's Daughter. Now the bands aren't quite so high-priced and the crowd is older, but there's still live music every night from Wednesday through Sunday. Tile dancefloor. A fine old traditional dance hall.

Helotes

An old village, eight miles northwest of San Antonio's Loop 410 on Highway 16, that dates back to Apache days when they and the Mexicans intermarried after picnicking and dancing there. Green corn dances were the rage then, and Chaca, the first resident, dubbed the settlement *Helotes*, which means green maize. Today, Helotes is still a social hub for commuters from the city and area farmers and ranchers.

FLOORE COUNTRY STORE AND DANCE HALL
Bandera Highway (16), Helotes

One of the greatest dance halls in Texas, bar none. Opened by John T. Floores in 1949, the indoor-outdoor store and stomp palace hasn't missed a high kick since. Floore's has three claims to fame. One is that Willie Nelson got his start there, one is that they've got the largest patio in the South, and the other is that there are more second-hand pickups in the parking lot than in all the junkyards of Texas. All are close to the truth. Willie did play at Floore's in the 1950's, and, after a hiatus, returned in the late '60s and early '70s for a one-night stand almost every month, even wrote a ditty to John T., who sold everything in his store from sheets to Shinola — that went like this:

> Now John T. Floores was workin' for the Ku
>   Klux Klan
> Six foot five, John T. was a hell of a man
> He made a lot of money sellin' sheets on the
>   family plan.
>
> *"Shotgun Willie"*
> *by Willie Nelson*

In 1973, John T. up and sold the place to Joe and Stella Algueseva, who had worked for him for 12 years. The Alguesevas and their brood have kept it a family honky-tonk. Kids are welcome with their parents. The store is open seven days a week. The dance hall Wednesday through Friday from 10 a.m. until 9 p.m., and on Saturday from 10 a.m. to 1 a.m. Sundays, 10 to 10. Live entertainment Saturday and Sunday, usually locals like the Metheny Brothers, George Chambers and the Country Gentlemen, Johnny Lyons and the Country New Notes. Once in a while stars like Barbara Fairchild will play, but Willie's too big now, too expensive.

In the summer the crowd moves outside to the patio and the picnic tables, but at the first cold spell returns indoors, where 400 can be seated. You'll find a mix at Floore's that'll bug out your eyes regardless where you're from. Good food. Homemade breads and tamales. Beer, byob, setups. No wine. And no green corn liquor unless you distill your own.

Schroeder

A 140-year-old spot in the chaparral northeast of Goliad formerly called Germantown, now a quiet clump of stores and ranch houses. Not far from the Fannin Battleground of the Texas Revolution and the old Spanish missions.

Lonesome country of hard-working folk until weekends, when everyone heads to the dance hall.

SCHROEDER DANCE HALL
Farm Rd. 622, south of Mission Valley and 15 miles northeast of Goliad.

As sweet and homey a place to dance as there is in Texas. I used to roughneck on a wildcat rig south of Yorktown, and every Saturday night we — the toolpusher, the driller and the rest of the crews who weren't working the graveyard shift — would head for Schroeder's. My cousins in the mesquite and cactus are still holding forth at the dance hall, which has been owned and run by Byron Hoff for 34 years. He's open only on weekends — Fridays from 8 p.m. until midnight and Saturdays from 9 p.m. to 1 a.m. — but Mr. Hoff hosts parties all the time on his off nights. He'll throw you a shindig for your wedding, anniversary, divorce, draft-call, whatever. A safe but fun place to teach the kids to dance. Schroeder's holds 400 at least and has a green oak dance floor which locals say is the best. Hoff's proud of his power plant which supplies AC and heat, and of the fact (he swears by it) that Roy Clark played his first dance *ever* at Schroeder Dance Hall for $50. "He had to beg me to come!" Byron Hoff says. You'll know the Schroeder Dance Hall by the big sign out front: a cowboy dancing with his lady. Local bands. A lot of oompah (still German country) along with C&W. Occasional big-name entertainment. Ray Price and Mel Tillis have recently appeared on special stands.

Bishop

This is a little grain sorghum and cotton town between Corpus Christi and Kingsville, only a few miles south of Driscoll and Robstown where I lived as a kid and first saw Ernest Tubb and Bob Wills at Rob's Place. That wonderful old dance hall has bitten the dust, but there was one outside Bishop that I found still standing and doing business. I could not believe that the gods would be so solicitous of such a modest, out-of-the-way saloon, and rushed in to have a cold beer and chat to make sure it wasn't a mirage.

The first time I had stood at the bar was on July 4, 1943. I was almost eleven. We had been visiting Uncle Earl and Aunt Arbie, who were living in a trailer house on the Armstrong Ranch out of Sarita (Earl was tool-pushing on a wildcatter), and now we were headed for a holiday of fishing and swimming at Aransas Pass. Earl and Arbie came with us. It was hot and we stopped for beer and soda pop at the Cotton Patch. I remember standing in the shade of the doorway, waiting for Earl to hand me one of those icy little six-ounce bottle Cokes, the kind that went down with a refreshing sting. The barmaid knew Earl. Hell, he was a big socializer. Said he had danced many a Saturday night at the Cotton Patch. All the way to Aransas we teased him about the barmaid being sweet on him.

The last time I had been at the Cotton Patch was in the summer of 1951. I was almost nineteen and had on my arm Nadine Ruggles, one of the most beautiful, honey-haired redneck girls I'd ever laid eyes on. We closed down the place drinking Cokes with bourbon and dancing to Hank Snow singing (on the jukebox) "I'm Movin' On." Now, here I was, back at fifty, the dark lovely Nanette on my old arm. We put a quarter in the juke and danced to John Anderson's "Wild and Blue."

COTTON PATCH
On corner of FM 666 and County Road 16 northwest of Bishop.

You guessed it. The Cotton Patch is in a cotton patch. There's sweet, white cotton and maize surrounding Polly Adams' place where bikers and farmers mix like honey and brown sugar.

The widow Adams has had the place for eight years now, but the building's been there nigh on 40. Twenty-five is a good crowd, except on Polly's birthday (September 10) when 100 of her friends gather. Polly's got Rex helping her out with the place. He does everything but tend the roses that grow 12 months of the year. That's Polly's department. Anyway, Rex liked the place so much he never went home and now lives in a trailer out back.

Polly lives in the bar and keeps the beer flowing, the jukebox playing and the pool table busy seven days a week. She doesn't just have country tunes on the box, but everything from Spanish numbers to even a little modern rock. But the music and the patrons all blend together. They'd better. Polly's six feet one and weighs 230 pounds. And this is the only beer joint for fifteen miles.

Edinburg

South of Raymondville, the country grows civilized again. The savage stretches of thorny brush peter out and give way to lush, green farmland terraced and tamed to the touch of a harvester's hand. Even the fences lose their barbed-wire bite. From field to field, as far as the eye can see, slender-trunked palm trees stand like stately sentinels on the boundary lines. This is the lower Rio Grande Valley, a 43,000-square-mile oasis where cotton and carrots and cabbage are kings over cactus, and the towns are strung together with a citrus necklace.

The Anglo is in the minority, but is content. He is the gentleman planter, the landlord and the employer. When he talks about the valley, he becomes almost lyrical, like Scarlet O'Hara singing of Tara. Smile, he says, you're in the Magic Valley. Sometimes it's the Golden Valley, the Miracle Valley, Eden and even Paradise.

When you put on blinders and look only at the Anglo's way of life, you can almost believe it. But there's another side, the valley the Mexican mockingly calls *La Valle Miserable.* It is the valley of most of the population, the border folk and the *cholos* who work the fields. Not even Appalachia is poorer. In no other place in Texas is there such a rigid caste system between race and class. It is a pyramid with the white planters at the top, a small middle-class of white and brown professionals and merchants and such, and at the great base the peasants.

Gringos of whatever status are in the minority, and there is little room in the economy for working whites, since they, like the Texas Mexican, cannot afford to pick in the fields as cheaply as the wetbacks and green cards (Mexican nationals with day-at-a-time work permits) the planters pick up at the border.

But this is not a social tract, at least not in *that* sense. I'm simply trying to be sociable and point out the honky-tonks, which, I must confess, is a waste of time this deep into Mexican Texas. The aristocratic planters don't bend to honky-tonk, and the Mexicans have their own dance halls. And since there are few rednecks down here, the pickings are slim. We found one outpost to our liking. As I said in the introduction many pages ago, there may be others, but I missed them.

SPLIT RAIL
1516 W. University
Edinburg

Manager Kenneth Brock insisted the Split Rail was "the last of the old-time saloons" in the Valley, and I know it's been around at least as long as the cure for Pancho Villa gonorrhea. That, incidentally, is a dip in Geronimo Springs, the hot springs just basinward of Caballo Fault in the Quitman Mountains on the Rio Grande between here and El Paso. A fur piece for ailments in Edinburg. But then there's always drink and more women and that's what the Split Rail offers. There's no cover charge for live music Thursday through Saturday by the Border Line. It's a rustic harbor for lonesome rednecks and ranch boys and their ladies. Larry Cade and Tom Eckles took over the place about eight years ago and revived it nicely.

Following The River Northwest

Back in my roughnecking days you could find some welcome if rough honky-tonks along the Mexican border, especially up around Zapata where the oil action was. But the exploration has pretty much played itself out. This means the oil patch people have moved on and have taken with them their honky-tonks. Still, it was worth a drive along the river up and out of the Valley. Nanette had never seen this part of the country. I made as our destination Brackettville and Happy Shahan's ranch and Alamo Village. That was more than 300 miles away, but the Buick was running well, so we took off up the river, following U.S. 83 through Rio Grande City, Zapata, Laredo, Carrizo Springs. As the highway veered away from the river, we cut back along U.S. 277 and hugged the Rio Grande through Eagle Pass, thence to Brackettville by way of Spofford and Ranch Rd. 131.

Happy Shahan is one of the great Texas characters. He, along with J. Frank Dobie and Graves Peeler, saved the Longhorn from extinction and brought it back to be a super breed. And in 1959, when Hollywood needed a place to film Lon Tinkle's book on the battle of the Alamo, Shahan built a mockup of the old fort-shrine north of Brackettville which still stands. John Wayne came and went but Shahan's Alamo Village is going great guns as a tourist attraction. There's a frontier village with a cafe and cantina that is a sure enough relief in that country because there is nothing else but western scenery.

Everyone at the frontier town was excited because Willie Nelson had just left after spending a day there taping a promotion for his new album, "Tough As Leather." Nanette bought some bandanas in one of the shops and we cranked up and headed for the border and Del Rio, where we'd heard there were some new honky-tonks.

The Buick came to a moaning halt over Pinto Creek five miles out of Brackettville. I had to leave Nanette in the car and walk back into town to get help. I knew what it was. The transmission which Lopez of Kaufman had newly sealed was dry as the creek bed over which we were stalled. I bought six cans of transmission fluid and hiked a ride. Nanette was composed. She sat reading *Midnight's Children,* a novel by Salman Rushdie.

"I'm sorry," I said, cracking open the cans of fluid.

"I don't care what happens as long as this novel holds out," she said, "It's one of the greatest things I've read in my life. Rushdie's a genius." And then she paused. "Too bad Lopez of Kaufman isn't."

I winced and went on about my business. I couldn't believe the seals in the transmission were leaking. I had watched Lopez put them in. But something somewhere had a hole in it. Full of fluid, but not for long, we limped back into Brackettville and began our search for Lopez of Brackettville. Nanette wanted me to try Garza of Brackettville or Martinez, anything but Lopez. But

I stuck to my allegiance to the Lopez name and tradition and found my man.

"Are you chure you wan' to feex eet, amigo?" Lopez of Brackettville said. "I doan know what to say, man. All I can say for chure is that theese car has seen eet's day, like you and me, man, that's for damn chure. Watch out, Pepe! Doan touch eet so hard. Eet might fall apart. What can I say, amigo? Maybe yes, maybe no. Come back tomorrow."

We got a room at the Longhorn Hotel. Nanette was so deep into the novel she didn't want to sightsee. So the next morning I borrowed a heap from Lopez and drove down to Spofford and into the mountains to visit an old friend.

* * *

Bois d'Arc Sam and the Cowpokes

A malevolent summer approaches in the rock-ribbed hills near the Texas-Mexican border. Windy portents of what is to come spin up and down the road to the mailbox, kicking up dust devils and shaking the mesquite. The bean pods chatter in the trees, and Father Castillo, the defrocked Spanish priest who lives beyond the canyon, likens them to castanets. But these are the Anacacho Mountains of Texas, not the Morenas of Andalusia, and Sycamore and I know them to mimic rattlesnakes.

I'm down to spend a day with the old prospector. He's rickety now, and everytime I see him I leave thinking it is goodbye, *adios, vaya con Dios, amigo viejo*. One day they'll call from Spofford and tell me he's been found dead in or around his shack, and that will be fine, as he wants it that way. He told me he'd just as soon they find him long after the fact, after his body is done with its fleshy decay and reduced to dry, beautiful bones, the Georgia O'Keeffe kind you stumble on in the desert.

Lonesome as this country is, Sycamore may get his wish. A phantom demographer passed through once and divined that if folks were spread out evenly you'd still have a mile between each nester. Sycamore claims there's no one within ten of him. Sycamore isn't rabid about it. He's even been known to take a drink down at the Cottonwood Inn, which is hid back in the brakes toward the Mexican border. And he went to Brackettville once to see Hollywood stage the Battle of the Alamo, came back with an autographed picture of John Wayne, which he keeps framed and hanging over his bed beside his certificate of membership in the Sir Walter Raleigh Pipe Smokers Club. That may not seem much to point to after a lifetime, but it represents something more solid than the mirage of gold and treasure that Sycamore pursued for so long.

One of the things that keeps Sycamore from winding down and expiring is his feud with Vince Witek, the mailman. It began when Sycamore made his mailbox too tall. Witek, who delivers in a panel truck, couldn't reach out the window and open the latch. He wrote Sycamore a note. Fix it, he said. Sycamore procrastinated. Prospectors are like blue-tick hounds. They are handy and resourceful when camped out on a hunt, but at home they are so shiftless and lazy they won't swat at a fly. Weeks went by.

Witek got tough.

"I will stop delivering your mail if you don't fix this mailbox," he wrote.

Sycamore hated to be intimidated by a civil servant, but when he didn't get his Sears, Roebuck catalogue he gave in and shortened the pole.

It wasn't long before Witek started complaining about the mailbox again, by note of course. He and Sycamore have never laid eyes on one another that they know of. Hope they never will. This time Witek said that besides being corny and pseudo Texasy, the horseshoes and spurs and saddlehorn Sycamore had sunk into the cement block which supports the pole were against postal regulations.

Sycamore was out removing the Texana when he got a funny feeling he was being watched. Sure enough he flushed a man from the underbrush. It was a one-armed black fellow, a rarity in that country (not the lack of a limb but the color), and Sycamore was a little wary until they warmed up to each other.

The stranger's name was Sam and he seemed as old as the first minnow in Tequesquite Creek, which is where he said he lived in a lean-to made of cottonwood saplings and coyote skins. He had an old dog with him and, yep, he called it Old Blue. The baby deer with the bell around its neck was called New Blue. Sam had a chaw of Bois d'Arc root between his cheek and gum.

"Say," Sam said "we could play a game of horseshoe pitchin' with them Texana," pointing to Sycamore's postal decorations.

"What are the stakes?"

"Loser has to lift the winner on his shoulders and carry him to Cottonwood Inn and buy him fo' shots of rotgut and put a nickel in the juke."

"Cottonwood Inn's too far to carry a man," Sycamore said. "Say the loser has to carry the winner to my truck, and we'll drive down there."

Sam didn't have but one arm, but it was long as Sycamore imagines Vince Witek's face is. And even standing behind the line, Sam could almost touch the far stake, so he got four ringers out of five and Sycamore got pretty close but that was all. "Okay," Sycamore said, hunkering down so Sam could straddle his shoulders. Sam climbed on, Sycamore stood up and staggered toward the truck, Old Blue following and after him New Blue, her bell tinkling.

Red Newt, the bartender, said he would serve Sycamore and Old Blue and New Blue, but that he wasn't gonna serve no you-know-what.

"I ain't a you-know-what," Sam said.

"If you ain't, then what are you?" Red said.

"I'm a Ethiopian."

"What's that?"

"Somethin' better'n a redneck," Sam said.
Sycamore may be a Robinson Crusoe of sorts, but Sam sure ain't no Friday.
"Well, you don't look no better," Red said.
"Have you ever seen a you-know-what with black teeth?" Sam said.
"Naw. A you-know-what's got white teeth, real white," Red admitted.
"Well, looky here," Sam said, grinning broadly.
His teeth were black as Bois d'Arc root.
"Awrighty, come on in," Red said, "but keep your mouth open so's ever'body can see your teeth."
Sycamore said they walked in and Lillie Belle McAlister looked up from the pool table and said, "Gawd, would you fellers look at that Ethiopian with the black teeth!"
He said Red smiled happily.
He also said Sam got 'em drunk and took all their money at 8-ball. It's easy to see how Sam managed to keep grinning.
I'm inclined not to believe a word of it. That country and all that solitude does something to a man's head. Which I like. And need more of from time to time. So I guess I will believe it.

* * *

Bless Lopez of Kaufman's heart. He didn't screw up my transmission. His seals held. Lopez of Brackettville said all that was wrong was that some bolts were loose in the unit that cools the fluid as it circulates through the transmission. I must have driven through high grass or something. He tightened things up in no time and charged me $3.50. Of course, the hotel room had cost us $40, but we still felt fortunate.

Del Rio was a disappointment. We did find a lively dance hall in Uvalde, home of the immortal Dolph Briscoe, who was asleep at the wheel of Texas government sounder than any governor in memory. His hometown was jumping, though.

THE PURPLE SAGE
Hwy. 90 west, 5 miles out of Uvalde

The Purple Sage has so many owners in the band they have a hard time running the place for all the music they're making. Backing up lead singer Vale Rodriguez (Johnny Rodriguez's nephew) are Roy and Lavayne Johnston, Jimmy and Jackie Rutherford and Ken Ruth. They call themselves the Riders of the Purple Sage, but they aren't the same band as went by the name in the '60s. The Purple Sage in Uvalde has been attracting dancers for two years, on weekends only (Friday from 7 to 12 and Saturday from 8 to 1). They also host special dances. Kids are welcome with their parents.

When the Riders aren't playing, you might find someone like Mel Tillis, Ray Price or John Anderson on the stage. And Johnny Rodriguez does his nephew a favor every now and then, too. There are two bars and a dancefloor upstairs, two bars and a dancefloor down. You can't miss the place. It's a green metal building, all fenced in, and it's the only honky-tonk for miles.

CHAPTER 13

The Coast

Down there in Houston they're
  doin' the boogie;
They're rockin' on the heels
  of them cowboy boots,
They're spendin' them big
  bills on parking lot cheap
  thrills,
Doin' what it takes to feel
  good;
Drinkin' them longnecks,
Acting like a redneck should.

Cowboys in pickups,
The girls are not stuck up
Doin' the Schottische and the
  Cotton-Eyed Joe;
And the music it just stopped;
He flew through the jukebox
Doin' what it takes to feel good;
Drinkin' them longnecks
Actin' like a redneck should.

Drinkin' Them Longnecks
by Johnny Slate, Danny Morrison
and John Wesley Ryles

Houston

Houston was a wicked city, and I was a wicked boy.

Houston was a wicked woman, and I was a wicked boy.

She steamed and teemed with life, laid up there in her bayou like some tropical trollop, and she took on all comers. I was but one of hundreds of thousands, and yet she wore me out, tender sprout that I was. In Houston I found nature in one of her extravagant moods, planting water palms beside desert cactus, mixing her metaphors, shaking up sea salt and chili peppers in the same salad, brewing up hot, humid Sundays and monsoon Mondays, pouring upon our fevered souls all the excess of Eve in Eden.

There was too much water and too much heat, too much humus and too much shade, too many flowers and fern and fruit and flies, too much blooming and too much fading and too much mildew and rot, too much hunger and too much gorging, too much thirst and too much drinking, too much music and too much dancing, too much sex and, finally, too much exhaustion and guilt.

I felt like Solomon. I pulled back a bit. The wine of it all was no longer intoxicating. My mouth was dry and bitter. Intemperance had done me in. Such feasting called for fasting and penance. I looked to the city to wind herself down, to cool off and permit us rest. But on she went. So I left.

I went down to the desert and paid for my sins in the malevolent sun and the high, hard mountains.

That was years ago. I didn't return until I met Nanette and became part of her family there. The city had changed. It had gotten monstrously bigger and that much more wicked and wild. So it is appropriate that the world's raunchiest and most raucous and most famous honky-tonk would find itself in the roughest, most redneck suburb of Houston. Houston probably has more honky-tonks than there are in the rest of Texas, but when one stands out from the others in the bizarre way that Gilley's does — while encompassing them all — there's no need to describe any but the big one.

GILLEY'S
4500 Spencer Highway
Pasadena

Gilley's wasn't always Gilley's, believe it or not. When I was a wicked boy reporter there a thousand years ago, it was called Shelly's, after the owner, Sherwood Cryer, a tough but straight-dealing welder who had turned club owner in spite of his aversion to drinking. Cryer owned more joints on Spencer Highway than you could make in a night. He sold beer and liquor and ice and groceries and ran the biggest vending machine business in South Houston. Shelly's was his most famous club. It was a big slab of concrete with a tin roof and corrugated iron walls that rolled up on hot nights. Over the bandstand was a parachute. There were two outdoor shithouses and a picket fence around the place. But he packed the kickers in, the petrochemical cowboys from the refineries along the ship channel. It was as hot a spot as you could find for country music fans. Cryer booked in Charley Pride, Bob Wills, George Jones.

Shelly's has been through three transformations.

The first took place when Cryer decided to go in with Mickey Gilley. Gilley had been playing in every joint but Cryer's along the Spencer Highway for twenty years. He had made some records but he hadn't hit it big. He was very big on Spencer Highway though, and when he and Cryer became partners, Shelly's became Gilley's with a new face and roof and an even larger clientele. While Mickey brought in the customers, Cryer managed Mickey's career right on up to the big time.

The second change that came over the club was after September 12, 1978, when *Esquire* magazine came out with a cover story, written by Aaron Latham, on Gilley's called, "The Ballad of the Urban Cowboy: America's Search for True Grit." This was followed by the movie, *Urban Cowboy*, which forever connected John Travolta with the dancing and the mechanical bull riding at Gilley's. The film, a worldwide hit, brought the beautiful people out to Spencer Highway in search of Texas Chic.

But Cryer and the club got over it. And that was the third transformation. Coming back down to good old Gilleyrat earth.

The night Nanette and I were there, we went with her cousins, Margie and Doug White, and we spent as much time gawking as we did dancing. I have never seen such a place, and such goings on, ever in my life. Dancing to the house band, The Bayou City Beat, is not necessarily the first or last or only order of activity. You can drink from several bars and watch the girls. You can eat at the cafe. You can put your quarters in more slot machines and video games than they have in the biggest arcades. They literally rim the dance hall. There's pool, shuffleboard, the mechanical bull, all sorts of carnival games against which you match wits and muscle. You can buy t-shirts, garters, suspenders, have boots custom-made and cowboy hats crushed to suit you. You can buy ropes and saddles and other rodeo paraphernalia. You can even go out back and watch a real cowboy rodeo in the arena next to the dance hall. Cryer has hundreds of signs blinking at you to buy this, buy that, or come to hear Mickey himself, in for a special stand, or if it's not Mickey it's Jerry Lee Lewis, David Allen Coe, John Anderson, Floyd Tillman, or whoever. There's a monthly *Gilley's* magazine, several newsletters, fan clubs for every singer nursed by Gilley and Cryer — Johnny Lee, Wendel Adkins, Steve Michaels, etc. — and even a recording studio, two record labels, two music publishing houses, and the devil and Sherwood Cryer know what else.

We went on a weeknight when there was no star performing and found the place overrun with sailors from the *U.S.S. Houston*. The mechanical bull was pitching them off as fast as they could climb on, a sight which the veteran toro riders found amusing. But the best people to watch were the regulars, Sherwood's shitkickers, the rednecks who had come out of the Piney Woods to work the port and chemical plants of Stinkadena, as they call the sweet smell of pollution around Pasadena.

When I was there dancing with them twenty years ago, they weren't into the cowboy hats the way they are now, but they were nonetheless country boys come to the stinking city to make some money and have a rambunctious time. In that they haven't changed. They are as colorful and bawdy as the Elizabethans who ate and drank in the penny gallery of the Globe Theater and threw ale and epithets at the villains in Shakespeare's plays. Gilley's is their theater and they, as much as the performers on the bandstand, are the actors. *Esquire* writer Aaron Latham was a bit put off by their cowboy costumes, since they grew up in a city of a million and a half people, but another writer, Bob Claypool, understands them better. If there is a bard for Gilley's, Claypool is its Shakespeare. Music critic for the *Houston Post*, Claypool was country long before Barbara Mandell claimed to be, and he knows his honky-tonks and his tear-in-the-beer music. In his book, *Saturday Night at Gilley's*, Claypool writes of Latham and the Gilleyrats:

"It seemed to irritate him that these cowboys lived in the city and didn't really ride a range — he never, for one moment, considered the fact that both groups, old and new, were simple country-bred white men who were doing the best they could at the only jobs they knew (and hoorawin' it on a Saturday night.)"

Claypool went on to observe that "The matter of internalized roots and following your heart's call seemingly never crossed Latham's mind."

But enough of writers and definitions. That's hardly what honky-tonking's about, and certainly not Gilley's. Let's leave it with Claypool's apt description. Gilley's is "The biggest, brawlingest, dancingest, craziest honky-tonk in Texas!"

Galveston

The old island isn't as much fun as it used to be before they cleansed it of sin. I liked it better in the days when a character named Clough was the mayor. When he was asked why didn't he do something about the prostitution on Post Office Street, the mayor allowed as how he was no match for Christ, and that since Jesus hadn't stopped prostitution there didn't seem to be any hope of anyone else doing it.

JIM'S COUNTRY AND WESTERN CLUB
510 Seawall, across from Stewart Beach
Galveston Island

This used to be Bob's Country and Western Club before Jimmy Jones bought it. It is the only honky-tonk on the island. Looks like a red barn from the outside, and it's big inside — 7,000 square feet. Jim has a mechanical bull, a thirty-foot bar, but the main attraction is all that room to kick to Silver Ranch, a fine and tight house band. Theme nights are popular. There's Pajama Night. You can get three brews for one if you wear your jamis. Jim's thinking about having Men's Jockey Underwear Night if he can get the real cowboys to do it.

"Are there any real cowboys out there on the beach?"

"Sure," Jim said. "They've just traded their horse for a surf board."

Jim's is open seven days a week, 5 p.m. to 2 a.m. Seats 400. If you can't get in, you gotta go all the way to Pasadena to country dance.

VRAZEL'S
On County Road 171 northeast of Danbury

For a true country dance hall, Vrazel's (pronounced Vrauzjulz) is at the top of the list. Only open on Saturday nights, Vrazel's features local bands like Kelly Nolan and Southern Tradition for $4 a head. Kids are welcome with their folks. Vrazel's has been a family-run establishment for almost twenty years, from the day they converted an old church into a country dance hall. They serve beer, but it's byob. The place opens at 7 p.m. and dances start at 9. Vrazel's can accommodate 300, so get there early. And if you have a benefit or bazaar that needs hosting in the area, Joe Vrazel will be glad to have it there.

DOC HOLLIDAY'S
5820 S. Staples
Corpus Christi

Doc Holliday's is a locally-owned-and-run honky-tonk in Corpus, and it's going out after a newcomer in town, Dallas. Billy McEntire, manager, said Doc Holliday's closed for remodelling just as Dallas came to town, and he has reopened with the "record longest bar in Corpus. I don't know what the record is for the longest bar in Texas, but we have a helluva long bar."

Doc Holliday's is in a shopping center, so it doesn't look like much from the outside. It seats 200, with an additional small bar and gameroom off to one side. You can dance seven days a week to house band Gunshy and an occasional rising star like John Anderson. Doc's has a mixed crowd between the ages of 21 and 45. As McEntire puts it, "Everybody was thrown off-kilter when we closed to remodel. They wondered if we were really going to reopen or if we were going rock 'n' roll. We're not. And we also believe in live music. Country & Western Music has always been stable in Texas — and it's never been a *fad* in South Texas."

CHAPTER 14

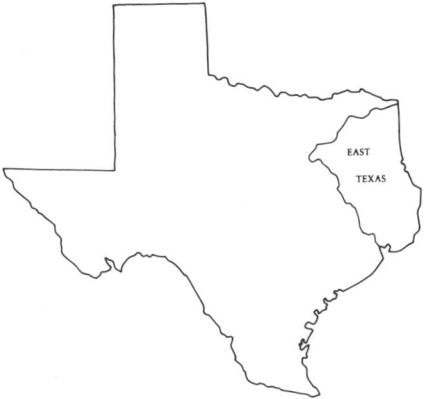

East Texas

Remember my talking about the Balcones Fault and how it creates a split personality in the lay of the land that is Texas? It runs up the center of the state on a north-south line. To the west of the escarpment stretches the ranch country where the rolling prairie rises onto the high plains, which in their turn bump into the rump of the Rocky Mountains. Out there it is hot and arid. The towns and cities are isolated and, of course, so are the people. There's no part of Texas which is drier, in every sense of the word. West Texans (most, that is) don't drink and they don't play. It's too damned hot. About the best you can do is put a cow out to pasture and hope she survives the hard winters and searing summers. That and read the Bible. To the east of the Balcones Fault lie a land and a people different from those to the west. This is the farm country and the shade of the woods. It is rolling to flat, a plain of post oak and then pine, a place of rich and fruitful soils, soft and Southern in its sensibilities. It contains most of the towns and cities and most of the population. Blacks almost outnumber whites. And as you get deeper into the woods, northeast of the Trinity River bearing toward the Louisiana and Arkansas borders, you know you are in another country.

    The feel now is one of a forest closeness. The sky isn't so all-fired big. Moss and frond thrive in the Gothic gloom of long-leaf yellow pine and post oak and a variety of other timber. Secluded farms and shacks are everywhere. It is a secret place where dappled shadows play, where woods hold gloomy grottoes and great houses hide obscure rooms and hushed stories, where black faces blink on bannistered porches and the roads out back run red as a rooster's comb and lose themselves in foxy fern. In the Texas plains, morning comes with a vivid, almost intrusive burst of light. The sun is out early with arson in its heart. But here in East Texas, the sun seems almost subdued, and if not that, then benign, as it enters the sanctuary of pine and dogwood. Here nature is dark, and light is induced, reluctantly, like a bulb on an aging actress' vanity, an intruder which is easily absorbed by the closeness and clutter of forms. The maidenhair is prayerful and the dew is longer on the leaves. It is a garden. Here people nest. Nature coaxes you to plant the seed of yourself as well as that of the melon. It is a place for the seedy and the fruity, the savorer and the secret drunk, which is why there are more porches and poets in East Texas than anything else. One could swear that Faulkner walked here and called it Yoknapatawpha. In a way his kith and kin did. A spattering of Sartorises and a wave of Snopses came into the country long before the Civil War, along with their blacks, and they still abide.

Folks in East Texas put the quietus on things — scandals, liquor and good times. That is, the whites do. The blacks have a world unto themselves that is freer and not so uptight about skeletons in the closet and mixing river bottom dance joints and Sunday-go-to-meetin'-de Lawd arbors in the same thicket. Whether jive, blues or gospel, the music that comes out of Black East Texas is rich, indeed, but since we are concerned with honky-tonks, a poor white foolishness, we'll have to pass over the most satisfying and soulful culture East Texas has to offer. The honky-tonk pickings are bare. Look at the wet-dry drink map. When it comes to boozing and dancing, this is the most prohibiting country after West Texas, and even in its wet precincts offers fewer dance halls than the high plains. But there is one county, Gregg, that can lay claim to having one of the oldest and greatest honky-tonks in Texas. I have danced in the place since I was a kid and my pa was a roughneck in those woods, and I hope to keep going back as long as my bones will bounce.

REO PALM ISLE
Hwy. 1845 and 259
Longview

In 1975, the Associated Press picked the Reo Palm Isle as the best club in Texas. Carl Johnson, the owner for 14 years (the place has been there for 50) says it's getting to be quite a tourist attraction. CBS even gave the Reo Palm national coverage.

Carl can't think of any one reason the place is so popular. He guesses because it's been there so long. From the outside it's just concrete brick. No big sign. He has a hardwood dance floor. The walls are pine and carpet with Western pictures hanging on them. He serves beer and setups. BYOB. No one under 19 is allowed in the Reo Palm, but you'll see 'em all the way up to ninety, dancing away to the house band, Reo Ramblers. Reo Palm is open Tuesday through Sunday, 7 p.m. to 2 a.m. except Sundays and Wednesdays when it's open from 4 p.m. to 2 a.m. Cover is $2 except on Friday and Saturday when it's $3. Check your hats at the door.

CHAPTER 15

The Hill Country

We Texans always seem to come in on the tail-end of fads and fashions and states of mind which sweep the country. Haight-Ashbury had come and gone, Woodstock was a cliche for the classic hip happening, and yet there we were on Independence Day, 1973, marching down a hill country road with 50,000 children of God, on our way to Willie Nelson's Fourth of July Picnic at Dripping Springs.

No speeches were made, but it was a Texas flower child's answer to Darrell Royal's Saturday afternoon sell-outs at UT's Memorial Stadium. Coach Royal himself, a great fan of Willie's, was on hand with his lady. Of course, they had backstage passes and we motleys out front never saw them. One spy reported that the Royals sat with eyes closed and gas masks on — to miss the bare bosoms and the scent of burning grass — but tapping their feet and swaying to music same as everybody else. The music was just country enough to draw rednecks, and just rock enough to pull in every freak who ever head-quartered at World Armadillo.

In other words, it was a red-letter day for Willie Nelson, who had done as much for honky-tonk race relations as Charley Pride. In those days the hills were pocked with two distinct races — the goatroper and the potsmoker — but Willie had proven that out of their extreme differences they could come to a common denominator in music. It wasn't always good music to my ear, but it expressed the split personality of its folk.

The goatroper sang of being down and out on the road, or being down and out in love, and what gave him surcease was a lot of beer and a little Jesus. What gave him the gumption to go on was a slug of machismo mixed with a tear of patriotism, and the dream that someday he might make it big on the juke like Buck and Hank and George, and maybe move in on the likes of Loretta, or Dolly and Tammy, even live next door to Charley Pride. That wouldn't be bad, a neighborhood like that and Charley the only nigger for miles.

The freak sang of being down and out on the road, or of being down and out in love — as much with mankind as with a girl — and what gave him relief was a lot of pot and a little Jesus or some guru in a gold Cadillac. What gave him the spirit to continue was the belief that he was beautiful and right, and the dream that someday he might make it big on tape and rip off the record companies, maybe make a movie with Dennis Hopper and get to go to jail with Joan Baez's husband for some higher cause than just getting busted.

Take the banality and the sentimentality of the Nashville Sound and mix it with the beat and sonics of rock, and you had the duke's mixture heard at Dripping that Fourth a decade ago. Some of it was damned good. Almost all the name performers — Willie, Leon Russell, Waylon Jennings, Kris Kristofferson, Tom T. Hall, Sammi Smith, Billy Jo Shaver, John Prine — were hot as firecrackers. Even regional favorites such as Kenneth Threadgill and Steve Fromholz had their moments.

But it wasn't the music, in and of itself, that the kids came to get into. It was the scene. You could tell they had come because it was the place to be, that here was where it was happening, man, and that the misery of it was something you had to endure, just as you had to reach for the seven-dollar admission.

It was miserable because it was a brutally hot day in those limestone hills. It was miserable because there were not facilities to handle that many people. Two narrow caliche roads lead into the Burl Hurlbutt ranch where the concert was held, and because of lack of parking space, cars were lined up on both sides of both ranch roads as far back as the main highway — some three miles at least — and then for five miles in each direction along 290. This meant that thousands of people walked as much as a dozen miles along those dust-choked roads to get to the amphitheater, everyone packing coolers of beer and some carrying babies.

Once there, there was little relief from the sun except what you could throw up in the way of shade. Many people had come the evening before and had spent the night passing stories and marijuana around the campfires. It was a return to the days of the great unwashed, to the times of the Gold Rush shanty towns and the outlaw tent cities when America — even then — was in flux and folk were striking out for new ways of life. Because of their appearance, it was difficult at Dripping to separate the young men and women and their romping children from photographs of pioneer Americans. Longhaired and bearded and beaded, the men lay among their women like Sultans of the Southwest. They smoked and swilled beer and some of them dropped from heat exhaustion; others gulped salt tablets, and a few ate mushrooms which sent them to the first aid station violently ill.

It was a mess. I came across Al Reinert, a writer friend who had come from Houston for the picnic, and I said, "What do you make of all this?"

"I'm not sure," Al said. "Here, have a beer. Let's settle down and mull this thing over."

We sat back against a picket fence and drank beer and sweated. We smoked and grunted.

"I've never seen so much law in my life," Al said, jerking his head toward some men behind us. They were Texas Rangers, unmistakable in their guns and gabardine and Stetsons and the frontier manfulness they affect, and you could tell they were as amazed at the scene as Al and I. "I've also never seen so many potsmokers lighting up under our very noses," Al went on. "The law don't seem perturbed, especially. They must have orders to lay off. After all, it is Willie's day as well as the country's." We agreed that only Willie could have gotten away with such special dispensation. "Maybe it's not a bunch of shit after all," Al said. I thought the jury was still out.

One woman, who had been waiting in line for 30 minutes to use an outhouse, turned to the person beside her and cried, "Why are we doing this? It is such insanity!"

Perhaps romantic illusion would have best described it. Certainly it was a state of mind which allowed them to think they were having a good time, and they clung to it tenaciously, like lichen out there on those hot rocks, cheering their cult leaders on stage with a mass exultance that would brook no exception. I was uncomfortable as hell, amiss in all the homogeneity. But who was I to question their thing? Maybe the heat and the noise and the cramp and stench of so many sweating bodies soured me. Surely there is, for some people, a joy in being part of the crowd, of being of one mind and one emotion and one costume with your brothers and sisters. I guess I got hung up in the contradiction, which hung over the place like a pall. I wanted to accept them as they saw themselves — beautiful and free and returning to old verities and hand-crafted values — but I could not. It was either my shortcoming or theirs, and I was outnumbered, an outsider, an intruder, just as I would have been among Jaycees and Rotarians, and so I left.

But they remained way past dark, until a power failure knocked out the lights and the music, and it was a great success, in terms of turnout and profit and however else they gauge those things, and they did it again and again over the next several years.

Willie Nelson had started something in Austin, something writer Jan Reid aptly called "The Improbable Rise of Redneck Rock." Out of it came, singing and playing, Waylon Jennings, Jerry Jeff Walker, Doug Sahm, Michael Murphey, B.W. Stevenson, Ray Wylie Hubbard, Willis Alan Ramsey, Bobby Bridger, Rusty Wier, Kinky Friedman and others. It was wild while it lasted.

Five years. That was all. It blew over leaving Willie and Waylon famous and rich beyond the boundaries of Texas, leaving their sidekicks scrambling to make what they could with the leftovers. Most of the promising careers turned out to be flashes-in-the-pan, and it was back to the cheap old road and lousy club gigs for some disappointed souls. Still, the Austin thing did something for country music that Nashville could not do, and we are the fuller for it. Not only did it give a red-blooded rock shot in the arm to Country & Western, it brought in strong doses of folk and ethnic elixirs, and helped make the medium more supple and expressive of all the cultural elements that were at hand. It was not only a revolution, but a revival of old forms and old heroes. Hank Snow and other oldtimers were brought back before audiences at the Dripping Springs picnics. And you knew the circle was complete when Waylon Jennings sang that a dead man was really the king.

> Well the honky-tonks in
> Texas were my natural second
>   home,
> Where you tip your hat to
> The ladies and the rose of
>   San Antone.
> I grew up on music that
> We called Western Swing,
> It don't matter who's in
>   Austin,
> Bob Wills is still the king.

Austin

Willie's long gone, but "Austin City Limits," the Public Television music show, is still hanging on. And there's always the legislature and Scholz's Beer Garten and the University and Memorial Stadium, Scholz's Beer Garten and the capitol tour and now *Texas Monthly* magazine, and yes, for a long time, even way before Willie, there was country music and honky-tonking and Scholz's.

BROKEN SPOKE
3201 S. Lamar
Austin

The Broken Spoke is so much an Austin tradition that Lt. Gov. Bill Hobby and the 65th Legislature proclaimed it "one of the legendary houses of Texas entertainment." As a place for solons to repair to for relaxation, the Spoke probably ranks third on the all-time list after Scholz's and The Chicken Ranch at La Grange, made infamous by Larry King's romp, *The Best Little Whorehouse in Texas*. Since Marvin Zindler closed The Chicken Ranch, we'll proudly move the Broken Spoke into second place. Even if you're not in the legislature you can have fun at the old honky-tonk out on Lamar. Once the site of the old Al Erlich Lumber Company, the Broken Spoke was opened by Joe and Lena Baland and their daughter, and her husband, James White, twenty years ago. At first they thought of it as a cafe, but so many customers were tapping their feet to the country jukebox that the Balands and Whites added the dance hall at the back. For a while they got local bands to play for pass-the-hat money, but as the dances got crowded they went out on a limb and booked real pros like Willie Nelson for $800 — back in '68. Bob Wills showed up every time they hired him but once. And he never sang at the Spoke. He just played his fiddle and whined, "Take it away, Leon." Even after Willie Nelson became famous, he would come out and sing with his dad, the old Ford mechanic and fiddler who was a favorite at the Spoke. Some of the movie, *Honeysuckle Rose*, was filmed there.

Come for lunch or dinner. The front is still a cafe, decorated in red vinyl and wood paneling, and they do a land office business in chicken-fried steaks (serving 1,500 a week). It's a family establishment. "Your children are just as safe here as anywhere you could imagine," Mrs. White likes to say. She sees second generation Broken Spokers come in with their kids to teach them to two-step. There's video games and the pool tables are free. Plenty of plaques to read on the walls. One says that Governor Preston Smith honored Lena Baland as a yellow rose of Texas in 1969. Another reads: "The Broken Spoke has been privileged to host these Hall of Fame Super Stars: Bob Wills, Tex Ritter, Roy Acuff, Grandpa Jones."

Open Monday through Saturday. Sundays are for private parties. House bands rotate nights when the stars are not in town. Alvin Crow appears on Wednesdays, and on the weekends you can dance to Bert Rivera, Mesquite, and The Roadrunners. Beer, BYOB. "We have so many old customers who would get furious if they had to pay $2 for a drink," says Mrs. White. "So we leave well enough alone."

DOUBLE EAGLE
5337 Hwy. 290 West, Austin

Formerly the Silver Dollar South, the place has been out on the highway seven years. It's a yellow metal building topped with a big sign. They have name entertainment every now and then, people like Joe Stamply, Shelly West and Michael Murphey. The Double Eagle has special event nights (ladies' night, nickel beer night) and on these occasions they draw a college crowd. Usually the clientele is mixed, though children under 19 are not welcome. Manager Rick Sanso thinks of the place as old-fashioned because it has a wooden floor and pool tables. But they've also got five bars, mixed drinks and video. Seemed like a mixture of old and new to us. It is one of the fewer newer places in Austin that has stayed country-western. Owners are Minnesota Vikings quarterback Tommy Kramer, his brother, Mike, and Ronnie Roark. Open Tuesday through Saturday, 8 p.m. to 2 a.m. Cover varies, but usually $3.

Luckenbach

Luckenbach, Texas is probably not what you'd expect it to be if you only know it from the song. In fact, nobody remembers Willie, Waylon and the boys ever playing there. The ghost town is famous because Cathy Morgan, Hondo Crouch and Guich Kooch revived it in 1970, making the general store/saloon/dance hall one of the shrines of early Texas chic. It didn't hurt matters that Jerry Jeff Walker brought his mobile recording van out to Luckenbach to produce the album, Viva Terlingua. Oh, Luckenbach was jumping in the days when Hondo Crouch was alive and on hand as the mayor and foreign minister of the town. It is curious, the people and the cultures that have passed through that tiny place 10 miles southeast of Fredericksburg on Farm Rd. 1376. It was a Comanche trading post before Albert Luckenbach took over the store in 1849 and named it after his forefathers. The Comanches never gave the German settlers much trouble, although renegades masquerading as Indians gave the townspeople such fits they had to call out federal troopers.

It was to Luckenbach that Professor Jacob Brodbeck retreated in 1870, five years after his experimental airplane crashed in a field near San Antonio. A man ahead of his time, ahead of the Wright Brothers by 38 years, the professor is said to have launched several successful flights at Luckenbach before his death in 1909.

I first knew Luckenbach from an Ancel Nunn painting of the store and of its proprietor, Benno Engel, who had succeeded the Luckenbachs. I danced there a lot in the early Hondo Crouch days, and remember once during a Luckenbach weekend Jerry Bishop and Michael Murphey walking up to me and saying, "Billy, you'd better check your son out. He's up to his ears in outhouse shit."

Winton was nine that summer, a boy with a shock of yellow hair. I found him head-down in a one-holer, fishing with a wire hook for a camera that had fallen into the crap. He came up with it dripping and smelling just as I caught him.

"Please let me keep it, Dad?"
"Why in God's name?"
"I can wash it off."

He took it to a faucet and cleaned it enough for me to tell that it was a cheap toy, and I made him throw it back down the hole. To make up to him, we left the dance early that night and slipped out to the old cotton gin, long abandoned, and spent a delicious two hours walking and climbing through it in pitch dark.

LUCKENBACH DANCE HALL

The dance hall was built in 1880, and nowadays they don't have many dances there because the owners are trying to preserve the place. Watch for dances on holidays or around chili cookoff time (October). If you want to know for sure, call the general store at (512) 997-3224 and ask for Cathy Morgan or one of Hondo Crouch's daughters, Becky or Cris. Since Hondo's death, the girls keep a close watch on the wear and tear of the dance hall, since it is an important monument to honky-tonking in Texas. In recent times, Jerry Jeff Walker has returned to record another album there, and the PBS television show, "Austin City Limits," has been filmed at Luckenbach several times. Stars still appear when there's a dance. George Strait is an old favorite. Gary P. Nunn played the Ladies Champion Chili Cookoff this past year. The store is worth seeing even if there isn't a hoedown. Some of the items on the shelves date back to before Benno Engel's time. Store hours are 10 a.m. to 9 p.m. every day but Wednesday. Sunday they're open from 1 p.m. to 9.

New Braunfels

It was in 1953 that I embarked on my career, beginning as a reporter for the New Braunfels *Zeitung*. The bank of the Comal was a halcyon place to start poking your nose into other people's business. I arrived one spring Sunday on a bus, fresh from the campus of Southwest Texas State, so new and wet that I still had a year to go on my education. My employer was Frederick Oheim, publisher and editor of the *Zeitung*, at that time one of the few German-English newspapers left in Texas. Oheim and his wife met me at the station. I liked them instantly. They were big, vital Germans, thick as sausages. Oheim himself was a magnificent-looking fellow. He had a great, bony nose, a heavy mane of white hair and a voice that thundered like Beethoven.

They took me to a beergarten and we ate and drank and talked of books and music and people and the beauty of being writers with a license to taste all these things. As evening fell, Oheim hung a paw on my shoulders and said in his heavy way, "Billy, if you do well at the paper, you can make a good life for yourself here. This is a garden."

I was moved. Across the room sat four handsome German girls, blonde and bosomy, and I thought of drinking and dancing and marrying one of them and having ten kids and becoming the bard of New Braunfels. We retired to the Oheims' house for a nightcap, and sat until daylight listening to Wagner on the phonograph. That would become a habit. Sunday night Wagner at the Oheims'.

Two maids named Pauline and Hilda became a habit too, especially Hilda. She was the second-heaviest and second-pinkest woman I ever danced across a tavern floor. She was out of Rubens. But I lied and said she was a Renoir woman. One night I told Hilda:

"People used to look at Renoir's naked women and wonder how he could tear himself away from them and sell them. It seemed to them that he would feign to paint them forever. They would go up to him and ask, 'How do you know when you're through with a picture?' And do you know what he would tell them?"

"What would he tell them, Billy?"

"He would tell them that he knew he was through when he wanted to pinch them. Just like this!"

I would pinch her and Hilda would squeal like a pretty pig.

Pauline was smart. She knew all about Kant and Fichte, but Hilda was fun. We spent many a Saturday night at the dance hall in Gruene. Then there were the Sunday nights at the Oheims'. Mondays always came with a judgment clout.

I thought I was being paid $40 a week to report and write for the *Zeitung*. It turned out that Oheim expected me to sell ads as well for his little weekly. And he told me to cut my hair. I sat back in amazement.

"Look at your hair!" I said.

"Don't be impudent," he growled. "I have earned the right to be eccentric. You haven't. You're still a cub."

Week after week, I did not earn a penny for the paper. Mr. Oheim had to go out and hustle last minute advertising himself. "There's something wrong with your sales approach," he said. "Show me, how do you approach a merchant?"

"I go to each shop on the square, like you told me, and I walk in and ask the boss, 'You don't want to buy an ad, do you?' They always look at me in their square-headed way and say 'No.'"

"That's because *you're* the square-head," Mr. Oheim screamed.

Poor man. I was also a wobbly reporter and a scared writer, tight as lockjaw when I sat before the typewriter. The Tuesday meetings of the city council, which I had to cover, were a mystery to me. Half the time the members spoke in German, a language the reporter for the opposition daily had learned at his mother's breast. My stories reflected my confusion and uncertainty.

One Sunday the Oheims called and said they were not up to having me over for Wagner that night.

The next Monday Oheim looked up from my copy he was editing and said quietly across the room, "Billy, you are fired. Don't think cruel of me. I am doing you a favor. You will never make a newspaperman."

I didn't protest. He was right. He was an Old World perfectionist who thought that colleges would turn out hard, finished craftsmen. I was green, soft and sappy, daydreaming of Hildas and Paulines.

And there in fat, polka land, before that fat, polka man, I wept like a Greek. I felt like young Eumenes, who after one idyll thought himself a failure. I took the bus back to school, too ashamed to say goodbye to the fulsome German girls. Paradise had beckoned only to find me unfit. So much for the Bard of New Braunfels.

I grieved for about a week. You know how fickle youth is. But it was good and salty while it lasted, my breast-beating, and in its transport I lived and died a lifetime in the pink arms of Pauline and Hilda.

Now, thirty years later, I kiss the memory of Frederick Oheim and thank Woden that they conspired to oust me from that Valhalla. If I had married Oheims' business and tied myself to one of his plump Valkyries, I would be there yet, a restless boy lost in the obese husband, swilling beer and jousting rumps to the polka. And worse, I never would have lain in the beds of Beirut and loved the dark one with rose in her hair and jasmine at her feet.

GRUENE HALL
Four miles northeast of New Braunfels on Gruene Rd., in the old village of Gruene. Take I-35 to Canyon Lake exit (FM Rd. 306), go west, turn left at first crossroad (yellow flashing light at Hunter Rd.) A half mile to Gruene.

Gruene Hall (pronounced green hall) advertises as the oldest dance hall in Texas, which is debatable but not all that misleading. It is one of the oldest and finest country dance places in Texas, and hasn't gone a week without a dance since it first opened its doors at least 83 years ago. The National Historical Society was in Gruene recently and couldn't pin a date on the structure, but locals say the hall was there before the town was established in 1873 by Henry D. Gruene. The Handbook of Texas, a sober reference, insists that Gruene did not add the amusement hall to his town until 1900, when he also opened a bank, a gin and a lumber yard. This would make the 1880 dance hall at Luckenbach older. But what's the fuss? It doesn't matter. Gruene Hall is a classic spot with no sign of slowing down. And it's open when the hall at Luckenbach isn't.

The dance hall is in the middle of the charming town of Gruene, which has become a favorite with tourists fond of German colonial and Victorian architecture. There are craft shops, restaurants (catch lunch at The Gristmill), and the Guadalupe Valley Winery.

I like to dance at Gruene in the summer when they raise the plywood window flaps around the huge wooden floor. Nanette and I were there in March when the windows were down. We had driven over from Seguin with my father and my sister Joyce and her husband, Jimmy. That night Possum Gap was warming up for Asleep at the Wheel, and we all danced except for Daddy, who couldn't because he wore crepe sole shoes that wouldn't slide over the boards. He stood in a corner and chatted with Frank Schlather, a regular at Gruene since 1930. He and Frank had several beers, and Daddy figured that if Frank had had three beers in Gruene Hall every four days a week since 1930, as he claimed, then Frank had had 33,072 bottles of beer at Gruene, surely some kind of record. Looking at Frank's nose, how could anyone doubt it? It was a record in itself. On the way home, we all agreed that Daddy had to get him a pair of dancing shoes. Gruene was great, and only a few miles from Seguin. It's open Thursday through Sunday from noon until everybody goes home, and the cover ranges from $3 to $7, depending on the band. Joe Ely and Ernest Tubb are big draws.

Hunt

The upper Guadalupe is beautiful and inviting, and this little town has long been a shopping center for the tourists who stay at the summer camps at dude ranches. For years now, the Crider family has been among the most popular hosts of Kerr County, and a meal and a dance at their place is something to remember.

CRIDER'S CAFE
On Hwy. 39, 3.5 miles west of Hunt

Crider's Cafe is a red wooden building, and next to it is an outdoor dancefloor and next to *that* is a rodeo. All dances, as you might guess, are held outside. People can sit around at the picnic tables and park benches and watch the dancers or the rodeo, either one. Linda Lash, the manager, cooks up whatever she feels like — sometimes chili and tortillas, sometimes T-bones or catfish. Always hamburgers and other staples. She serves lunch and dinner Tuesday through Saturday, and then Saturday night they have the rodeo and dance until 1 a.m. They have different bands all the time, but most of them play swing, "like Bob Wills," she said. Wilton Crider is the owner, one in a long line of Criders who have run the place. Linda says she thinks the cafe was opened in 1925 or thereabouts, and now Wilton leases out the cafe and beer concession. The rodeo attracts cowboys from all over to compete for the purses, and thousands of folks — adults and kids alike — come to the dances. There's a long bar at Crider's that serves beer, and new this year — wine. Local photos and art are for sale. Crider's is a seasonal place — open only in the summer — but the Criders are thinking about keeping it open during hunting season this year. Look for special holiday rodeos (Fourth of July) in addition to regulars on Saturday nights.

* * *

Devil's Backbone

Eons ago, a great sea covered this part of Texas. Through the ages, the bones and shells of sea creatures settled on the ocean floor, building a vast plateau of limestone. At last, Edwards Plateau hove out of the sea. As it rose, it cracked on one end and a crevice ran up the center of the land. Springs gushed from the fault line, forming rivers and streams which coursed through the sloping country, cutting out canyons and gorges and basins. Today, this great crack, called the Balcones Escarpment or Balcones Fault in sober company and the Devil's Backbone by drunks, splits the state in half. East of the fault lies the flat farm country. The hilly ranch country rolls west. It was upon the humpy back of the devil that I learned one of the lessons of my life. It is simply that fat women are beautiful and among the most engaging companions a man could desire. The bigger they are the better. This I learned as a student in the hills.

But before I tell you about it, I have a confession.

* * *

Short in Texas

I am about to divulge something that no man in his wits would boast of, so please take it as a confession on my part and not some grotesque vanity. In a literal as well as a figurative sense I am removing my Adler Elevator Cowboy Boots and my high-crowned cowboy hat, I am standing here flat-footed and bare-headed, naked so to speak, to tell all that, midgets and dwarfs aside, I am one of the shortest men in Texas.

When Randy Newman sang his satirical song about short people he was describing Porterfield. I got little hands and little eyes. And I walk around tellin' great big lies. I got a little nose and tiny little teeth. I wear platform shoes on my nasty little feet.

Again, I take no pride in this divestment, for it shows me falling short not only in stature but in sincerity. For years I have lied about my height. And I have gone to ridiculous lengths to make myself seem taller. I have been quite good at this deceit, I must admit. People are endearingly gullible.

My masquerade as a medium-sized man has been complete and well-nigh foolproof, even down to maintaining a mild character. Have you noticed how abrasive and cocky, even downright obnoxious, short men are? Obviously they are compensating. Mine was subtler. I cast off that agitating aspect, and by the guile of disguise made of myself a moderate and most ordinary middleman. No one knew. Not my wives, my lovers, my friends, my children. I was clever to marry tall women. Not so tall that they had to pick me up just to say hello, but tall. And I was cleverer still not to try to make myself taller than my amazons, although I did wear socks with secret lifts to bed. A bit eccentric, yes, especially for a man who is trying not to draw attention to himself, but the first two spouses thought I had cold feet and the last one came close in attributing it to compensation, although she had the reason wrong. She thought I had bald heels and didn't want her to know. I let her think that. And indeed it was true. I have no hair a'tall on my heels. But I've never been uptight about it.

Why, after all that contrivance, do I now reveal that about which I was so sensitive? I wish I could give it a noble, even sacrificial motive — that somehow future generations would be enriched by my penance — but such is not the case. The plain truth is that I grew tired and could not keep it up. The times caught up with me. Can you imagine my frustration when other Texans, already out of my reach, began to go crazy over cowboy boots and make of old Charlie Dunn and Sam Lucchese cultural heroes to match Willie and Waylon? The music fit has died down some but you can bet your boots the run on high-heels is no spur of the moment thing. Today it is depressing for me to pass a shoe store. If it isn't boots it's platform shoes. Everybody is elevating! Adler's secret is out and we short people no longer have a built-in advantage. I have seen this coming for years, but when I broke my ankle dancing in my Top Secret Triple Decker Dude Ranch Specials I just had to face the fact that there are limitations on how high a man can go on artifice before he's due for a fall.

My Mexican bootmaker, who shall remain nameless, had actually crossed himself and muttered three Hail Marys when he inserted those last Icarus lifts. The inside of the boot looked like a staircase. I think he wanted to give me a parachute. But I was a desperate man. If I had to go out I wanted it to be on a high note. It was, dancing at Faces to Mother of Pearl. You see, I swagger like Yosemite Sam when I walk and on the dance floor I do a lot of jumping around. Chantal Westerman saw me dance one night and said I reminded her of a cricket. I mean, I am constantly hopping as high as I can. It is wearing and Christ it is dangerous on stilts, but it is deceptive and creates the illusion that I am larger than life instead of smaller. It seems to work because couples often stop dancing and stare at me as I hop about being larger than life. But that night I tried one herculean hop too many and had to be carried out. Since then I have hung up my tall tack and all that rigamarole and offer it to John Tower and Robert Mann if they will come down from Washington and pick it up.

Texas is distinctive in having created two types of expatriates: writers and short men. It is brutally indifferent to its bards and gives its short people the freak treatment. Small wonder that I was a closet munchkin, a phantom bantam. But at least I stayed and tried to deal with it instead of running off even though I was twice damned by being both a writer and a runt. Look at Larry King. He's long as loblolly and tall on talent but short on gumption and had to hightail it. And Bob Mann simply could not take the double disapprobation of being a whimp of a wordsmith. So he taught for a while and then struck off for the Potomac. Mann did stick around long enough to help me in my liberation from the Dachau of deception in which I had so elaborately imprisoned myself. And for that I am beholden. But looking back, I'm afraid the little man, Mann, while meaning well, made it worse for me to come through the rye of my revelation.

Dallas broadcaster Alex Burton is a big bearded man with a deep voice. If we lived in a mythological time when folk spoke metaphorically instead of specifically, I would not give you Alex's height in feet and inches or the timbre of his voice in decibels. I would portray him in hyperbole. Why, I'd haul off and say that Alex, who hails from the Canadian woods, is big as Silver Jack Driscoll, the late King of the Michigan lumberwood fighters. And Silver Jack could fell an ox with one hand and tie bowknots in iron horse shoes. And I'd cock an ear and allow that Alex's voice carries as far as Mills Darden's did. Mills was that acromegalic giant from North Carolina who could holler so thunderingly loud he could confuse a sunny heaven and make it rain.

That, incredibly speaking, is Alex Burton. And yet Alex is not intimidating. In fact he is funny, an accomplished radio wit and media savant who has become something of a celebrity in Dallas. I used to have a beard. I used to be on television. I too was a small-time celebrity. But I got fired. Alex is still on radio, but he's also on television now. There is little difference between Alex Burton and Billy Porterfield when Alex is sitting down and I am standing up, especially when I wore my cheaters. But there he sits before the cameras, minus the two telephone books I used to mount, getting all the glory and adulation the boob tube gives you even in a two-bit operation Neilsen never notices. Why? I ask. But this is rhetorical. I already know the answer. I blew myself out of the tub when I announced to the TV types that I was going to go on the air and confess to being a crypto short person. No, they cried, it would ruin my image. After all, my persona reflected on the station. Viewers would be shocked. I might as well have confessed to being an atheistic, bisexual leper. They dropped me quick and went looking for a more Texan-esque type and found him in Alex, Canadian accent and all.

The point is that it was Bob Mann's idea, after I had hung up my high heels, to make a big deal out of my being short. His reasoning was that mythical places such as Lilliput and Brobdingnag and Texas make men mad for extremes, and that if I couldn't be the biggest then damn it let me be the smallest, that one or the other stands out and is better than the middling mean that marks obscurity. Of course he didn't say it that way, but that's what he meant. Or did he? Maybe he just wanted company in misery. If you want to get technical about it, what Mann actually said was unprintable. Then he had another drink and smiled at me with glazed, slit eyes and slid under the table. But I clearly got the drift. We were banty roosters against the world. Trouble is, our caper backfired.

Alex I couldn't blame. He took what came, including the abuse Bob Mann and I heaped upon him later in front of the Dallas police station. Mann and I were waddling along Harwood when he spotted Alex standing on the curb waiting for a traffic light to change.

"Lilliputians to arms!" Mann shouted, and charged the startled Burton. Well, here again, I'm running away with myself and poetic license. What Mann probably said was, "Let's flatten the sombitch the way Dempsey did Firpo!" At any rate something stirred in me. Revenge. I joined Mann. We fell upon the giant Burton's legs, trying to bring him down. Traffic stopped. A crowd gathered 'round. We bowed our heads and butted at his shins. We growled and jumped up and down on his toes. We wrestled mightily but we wrestled for naught. Our Gulliver would not come down.

Alex looked at us curiously, then helped us to our feet and dusted off our clothes. He even picked up Bob and brushed a little tear out of his teeny little eyes. A policeman wanted to arrest us but Alex waved him away, saying, "Oh my good man, I cannot sufficiently wonder at the intrepidity of these diminutive mortals, who durst venture to mount and walk upon my body, while my hands are at liberty, without trembling at the very sight of so prodigious a creature as I must appear to them." Well, of course, he was right. We must have been insane.

What is left for me? Why, more masquerade, of course. But this time that of the fool. I have played one here with thee. Entreat me further to entertain. I am not a Charlie Chaplin or a Woody Allen, but I have my tricks. I know sayings. An Epigram? How about:

> What is an Epigram? A dwarfish whole.
> Its body brevity, and wit its soul.

Uncle Eddie Porterfield was a circus midget and used to being stared at. In fact, he invited it. But privately he hated it. It was one of Uncle Eddie's genuine resentments, the way heightism — a prejudice as strong as racism and sexism — infects even the language. A stupid person is short of hat size. People who lack foresight are shortsighted. A cheat is a short-change artist. When you are broke you got the shorts. You are a day late and a dollar short.

It wasn't just words. Heightism, Uncle Eddie observed, cut us down to size in business and politics as well as in bed. Tall men made more money and got preferential treatment. Americans preferred the tall man for president, movies and magazines touted the towering leading man, and not even Masters and Johnson could stop the snickering fallacy about phalluses. They had us, Uncle Eddie said, by the short hair.

And yet what sustained Uncle Eddie was his unswerving belief, based on considerable scholarship, that the small human being was superior, over the long genetic haul, to the large human being. He said nature realized this, and that in the beginning nature had made man too big for his own good and had since been whittling him down to a finer proportion. Of course this did not accord with our own family history — hell, we were getting bigger — nor with the vital statistics that showed a general increase in size in almost every generation in America and Europe. A momentary inclination, Uncle Eddie said, not amounting to much on the whole scale of human history. Scale was one of his favorite words.

I remember well our conversation. It was in the Continental bus depot in Corpus Christi, on a damp evening in the fall of 1950. I was a freshman at Del Mar Junior College and feeling pretty down-in-the-mouth because I hadn't been able to make the football team. The coach, Ox Emerson, had not even let me try out. He'd taken one look at me and laughed, "Charlie Dollar'd make two of you." Dollar was Del Mar's smallest back. So here I was living in the music dorm with a bunch of queers and sissies trying to make the choir for God's sake.

It had not occurred to me up to that time that I was all that little, much less too small to play football. Our clan was wee and I just assumed that everybody was as pint-sized as we and the Mexicans were. It made me mad later to read in the college library that Texans were the tallest Americans. An anatomy professor, Dr. Clarence M. Jackson of the University of Minnesota, had written in 1930 that "In stature, the tallest average is 68.4 inches in Texas, probably with largely nordic ancestry . . ." It was obvious to me the professor had not been south of San Antonio where the nordic gave way to the hispanic.

At any rate Uncle Eddie had been appearing with some carnival at the State Fair in Dallas and was just passing through Corpus on his way to Mexico for a honeymoon with his new lady, Tina, who had brought along her senile father, Roy, both of whom had been in the Guiness Book of World Records — Roy for being the worst driver and Tina for being fat. Roy had made it by getting 10 traffic tickets in twenty minutes in downtown McKinney, Texas, a *tour de force* that had caused the crackup of a dozen other cars. And all he was doing was driving to the post office to mail a letter.

Tina weighed 402 pounds. Uncle Eddie weighed 72. And he was fat. But he was kind and sought to soothe me, as I would later my own kid when he hurt from being so small. We sat at a booth in the bus station, Uncle Eddie holding forth with his chihuahua in his lap as we had coffee. He was done up in a nice little black suit that had to be custom-made. If he hadn't been so small you would have forgotten he was a circus freak and would have thought he was a foreign dignitary or something. He had even maintained his dignity when Tina picked him up like a doll and kissed him. Now she dragged her father off to the pinball machine to see the pretty, blinking lights.

"Look," Uncle Eddie said, "by not making the football team you have saved yourself from the gladiator ring. Don't get down in the pit with the brutes. Go up into the emperor's box with the brains."

Uncle Eddie paused and smiled and looked across the depot at Tina. She was about to destroy the pinball machine.

"I see what you mean," I said.

"Think of it this way," he said. "Size and primitiveness go hand in hand. Anthropology supports it and so does religious myth. The Bible says, Genesis 6:4, that 'there were giants in the earth in those days.' And Lord knows that antiquity is full of titans: Polyphemus, Goliath, Gargantua, Rubezahl, Gog and Magog. Science concurs. Two of our earliest specimens of men, the giant from Java — Meganthropus — and the giant from Hong Kong — Gigantopithecus — both were bigger than gorillas. In the human evolutionary line, the more primitive the forms, the more gigantic the dimensions. Early man was much bigger than modern man. And yet who would deny our superiority? Dear boy, remember the wisdom of Didacus Stella, who said that a dwarf standing on the shoulders of a giant may see farther than the giant himself."

Uncle Eddie went on to sustain his theory through the march of civilization. As human history evolved it was quite clear that the little man with brains had lorded it over the big man with brawn. Occasionally there were role reversals: the dwarf who played the house fool, the intelligent giant. But, Uncle Eddie insisted, most of the movers and shakers — Socrates, Hannibal, Caesar, Christ, Mohammed, Cortez, Voltaire, Rousseau, Napoleon, Franklin, Einstein — were physically frail types who had used their wits and courage and special gifts to prevail. Davids against Goliaths.

Churchill had been a marvelous example. Here was a small, sensitive boy, bullied and beaten at school, who grew up into what the poet Wilfrid Scawen Blunt described as a "square-headed fellow of no very striking appearance." Winston was short and fat. He had a chicken chest with no hair on it. His arms were thin and his hands were a woman's. He spoke with a lisp and a stutter.

"So you see," Uncle Eddie said in summing up, "we have in Churchill an endomorph with a pronounced proclivity for somatotonia."

"Which means?"

"That he had the body of a mouse and the temperment of a lion. It was this very conflict in his own nature that drove him to greatness."

Well, that was all I needed. An heroic model. On campus I went about as Sir Winston. I adopted his waddle walk. I bent my head and went about scowling with bulldog defiance. I gave the "V" for victory before there was a soul handshake and I spoke with what I considered to be Churchillian cadence on appropriate circumstance. It would not have been so odd if I had been matriculating at Oxford. But here I was flunking at Del Mar Junior. But I stayed within the character I had adopted. When Prof Kelly, old Paramecium John, caught me cheating on a test in biology he demanded to know what I had to say for myself. I intoned:

"I have nothing to offer but blood, toil, tears and sweat."

Dean St. Clair took it out in blood, after which there were considerable tears and sweat, for I found myself expelled.

Charlie Camp, a tall, easy-going classmate, wrote in my annual:

"To a fine little shrimp, but try not to be so salty."

And Uncle Eddie wrote from a circus wagon in Florida:

"Being short and sassy isn't enough. You have to be smart too." Well, that was asking too much of me, even at Southwest Texas State where they took me in.

* * *

San Marcos is a lovely hill country town but the college in those days was hardly a Platonic dream. Years later one of its presidents would cause great embarrassment to the Texas academic community when it was discovered that he had pirated his Ph.D. thesis from other sources. Up to my time there the institution had produced Lyndon Johnson and several generations of goat ropers. We all wore 88-pound belt buckles and 10-gallon hats. I quickly wore out my welcome in the hard disciplines — mathematics and science were lost causes as were most of the required courses. Failing that I faked my way through easy electives and became something of a misfit. If I couldn't be smart I could be poetic and profound. I grew long hair and smoked a pipe and spoke only in aphorisms and epigrams, none of which were original on my part. When my dorm mates would lounge around Ward Hall drinking Lone Star and eating cabrito (a stolen goat Slim Felps had slaughtered and smoked and kept hidden in a basement refrigerator) and praying for peace because they were afraid they were going to be drafted into the Korean Police Action, I would still them, I would throw them into a brown study with something like:

> "Peace is but invisible war in which nations rest only to
> fight again."

Of course I would not give Will Durant credit.

To the shit kickers I was a real deep little man, no matter that my grades were sorrier than a cedar chopper's word. I spent three years in those hills riding around on the shoulders of my giant rednecks, spouting the great quotations and drinking brew at Be-Back's and O.S.T., short for Old Spanish Trail, where all the Mexican cantinas were. It was in the Devil's Backbone Tavern on Highway 12 that I, like Uncle Eddie, found my Tina.

Actually I met her at the college in San Marcos. One Saturday night in Ward Hall we boys were wanting to go dancing but every girl we knew was busy with some other fellow. Since I was the best word man among the lot of us, I was chosen to call the Co-Op and see what I could rustle up there. The Co-Op was an outcast dorm for poor girls and misfits who could not afford to live in the sorority houses and wouldn't have been asked if their daddies had been rich as H.L. Hunt. It was high on a hill away from the campus. This was the last place you would look for a date, so you can see how desperate we were. Actually, my brother had been dating girls at the Co-Op on the sly, and he went around with a grin on his face as if he knew something we didn't. As it turned out, he did.

I got the Co-Op switchboard operator on the line and asked her if she knew of any girls that were hanging around wishing someone would call and ask them out. I knew that the operators were students themselves, making a little bread on the side.

"I certainly do," she said brightly. "I get off in 30 minutes myself, and I'd love to go dancing. How many more girls do we need?"

"There's five of us," I said.

"I think I can do it," she said.

"Great," I said. "How do we choose sides? You know. Who gets who?"

"Let's you and me settle it right now, or else it could get sticky and awkward, and someone would get their feelings hurt."

"That's a good idea," I admitted. "Say, what's your name?"

"Jessie."

"I'm Billy. Jessie, I like the way you talk. Why don't we couple up?"

"Fine with me. Now that that's settled, tell me about the other four boys and I'll try to match them with the right girl."

"You got that much to choose from?"

"You're telling me? It's the pits tonight. Everybody's sitting around here with their hair in rollers."

"Okay. There's Charlie Crowell. He's a big, burly guy, yellow-haired and blue-eyed. Quiet, nice, kind of shy but solid. He's sort of our bodyguard."

"The strong, silent type. I know just the girl for him."

"Yeah? Charlie'll appreciate that. Then there's Goode, Donald Goode. We call him Dad Goode because he's bald and old enough to have been in World War II and the Korean War. He's kind of a misanthrope, really a recluse until he gets a little beer in him, and then he goes wild. He's not handsome, but he's smart."

"Nice personality?"

"No."

"Dad Goode may be tough to match. But I'll try."

And on we went.

Before I hung up, I asked Jessie what she looked like so I would know her when I saw her.

"Lord," she said. "I'm as big as the side of a house. I'm closer to six feet than five and I weigh as much as a guard on the Bobcats."

"I can't believe it!" I said. "Your voice makes you sound like a tiny little thing."

"No. I'm fat and I've got freckles. But I'll dance your legs off. Still interested?"

"Hell yes, woman. That is, if you'll take me. I'm a short guy, closer to five feet than six. But I love to dance."

"Get on up here, Billy," she said. "I can't wait to see your little butt."

It was the beginning of a great friendship. I've never had so much plain old fun in my life. No lovey-dovey, no complications. Just high times and affection. She was a going Jessie, Jessie was. A sport. Prodigious drinker and dancer and yet never a slob. A Bohemian milkmaid who in her opulent pink flesh and freckles was truly worthy of Ruben's brush. She wasn't carnival fat, but she was heavy enough to make the jukebox roll toward us when we danced near it. We'd dance away and it would follow us. I wanted Uncle Eddie to meet her. I wanted him to see me in my new element as the elf of Epicurus, complete with my outsized queen and court of fools. He would be flattered by my imitation, for of course Uncle Eddie was my model, my mentor. We exchanged letters. We made arrangements. He and Tina and Roy and the chihuahua would come. They would catch the Continental.

But it never came to pass.

One night in their trailer in Florida, Tina, inebriated to the point of insensibility, rolled over in her sleep and crushed Uncle Eddie's chihuahua to death. Uncle Eddie was equally crushed, his heart that is, and he could no longer find it in himself to love Tina. After burying the chihuahua in the cutest little casket at Three Ring Paradise Memorial Park, which is a kind of Valhalla for departed circus folk, Uncle Eddie gave Tina her walking papers. He wrote me, "That goddamn Didacus Stella forgot to mention one thing. Never ride a giant that's been drinking. You can get killed that way."

But I would not be deterred from Jessie. We danced away the semesters on Devil's Backbone, and when it came time for her to leave (she was a year ahead of me), Evelyn Kubina, the hostess at the tavern, helped me throw a farewell party. We had a beery good time. I promised Jessie at the door of her dorm back in San Marcos that if I ever got in the marrying mood I would come looking for her. She laughed and kissed me and we parted and I never saw her again. That's the way it is when you're twenty.

The other day, broke down in the hills and waiting for Paul to send Lopez of Wimberley a water pump for the Buick, Nanette got restless. So I borrowed Daddy's 1957 Ford pickup and we drove out to the old tavern on Highway 12, which runs right up the spine of the devil. I had not been there in thirty years, but everything looked exactly the same. I swore to Nanette that the same records were on the jukebox. I petted it and said it was the very one that had followed old Jessie and me around the dance floor. No No was not particularly touched. "Come on," she said. "Let's get back to Wimberley and see if Lopez has the Buick ready."

"Let me just see if that's Evelyn Kubina behind the bar," I said. "It looks like her.

"No," the old woman said. "I'm not Evelyn. She sold the place to me some years ago. But she's still around somewhere in these hills."

"I could swear that was Evelyn," I kept saying on the way back into town. "If she wasn't, she was a dead-ringer, that's for sure."

"Yeah," Nanette said. "And the next fat woman we meet will be Jessie. You old sentimental fool!" She put her foot so deep into the carburetor that Pa's pickup shuddered and actually got up to 31 miles an hour.

* * *

The Last Dance At Red's Place

Red Casparis was an oil tool salesman until the day the big boss from Houston caught him drinking on the job. So he came back to Johnson City and opened a beer joint on the square behind the courthouse.

Red could have gone somewhere else and made more money. That's not because people around here don't like beer. Red said where you find domino players you find beer drinkers. Trouble was, there weren't a lot of people left around to buy it. The population of Johnson City was down to 611. In fact, the whole county's population had dropped over the last three census counts. Everybody was hoping that things would perk up now that Lyndon was president, but Red hadn't seen any signs of a lasting influx of folks. Once in a while the press and the Secret Service agents would drop in to sip a cool one, but the tourists stayed away. "I guess it's my rustic decor," Red supposed.

So it was quiet around the square, not exactly a businessman's bonanza. Red came back because he felt like somebody had to look after his mother and daddy, who were up in years. The nine other Casparis children had moved away.

Red was trying to make the best of a sleepy situation. For a year, he'd been mulling over the idea of opening a dance hall in the room behind the bar. One July night he tried it.

He got a band out of Austin to agree to play for 70 percent of the gate. The bandleader, a Black hipster by the name of Roper, wanted a guarantee. Red wouldn't give it to him. He wasn't sure ten people would come.

By dance time, twenty-one men and two women had showed up, but no band. Everybody waited around for an hour. Red kept looking at the Pearl

Beer clock on the wall and mumbling. He'd advertised the dance all over the county, went to a lot of trouble getting tables and chairs and a license. The customers, weary of waiting for a band that apparently wasn't coming, began leaving. As they filed out, Red refunded the seventy-five cents he had charged each of them at the door.

Wes Waugh, 82, couldn't hide his disappointment. He had mentioned the dance to everybody he met all week and had even gotten a haircut. The barber, Pancho Althaus, had come with him. Now Wes said he wanted to go home. He was sick to death that the party had fizzled. Naw, said Pancho, stick around, I'll dance with you. Wes gave him a sour look, but they joined Red's cousins at the domino table.

They were shuffling the dominoes when the band arrived.

Roper said he was sorry. He had to scramble to get a drummer, and they'd gotten lost on the drive from Austin. Red grumbled a little, but told Roper and his boys to go ahead and start playing. Maybe the noise would wake up the town to the fact that there was going to be a dance after all.

Red knows his people. It sure did. And it turned out to be a fairly profitable night for Red. The crowd drifted back, and by the time the dance really got underway there were five women — counting Red's lady — and about thirty men.

Most of the men didn't dance. There weren't enough women to go around and the band was grooved in the rock 'n' roll style. Rock didn't make much sense to Johnson City polka dancers. As Wes Waugh said, "Why ask a woman to dance if you're not goin' to hold onto her?" But Wes and the barber didn't waste time when the band played an occasional slow piece. Wes danced with Betty, Red's girl, and then Pancho gave her a swing while Wes boldly pulled a fresh-faced blonde around the floor. He'd been itching to dance with the blonde after he watched her twist with her boyfriend, a callow youth nobody knew. Wes said she "wiggled ever little ole thang." Somebody said she looked like the Harvey girl. No. The Harvey girl was a little lighter in the ankle. Besides, the Harvey girl *sure* wouldn't make a public exhibition of herself. This gal was from across the county line, had to be. She was a cutey though.

Red sold a lot of beer — more than he would have sold on a routine night — and he got almost eight dollars of the gate. He said he'd try it again — with a different band — if he could find a group who'd play without a guarantee. Roper and his boys said they wouldn't come back if Red wanted them, which he didn't. Their take of the gate — and their take for the night — was eighteen dollars. Split that five ways and a man wondered if they even made expenses. They drove from the capital in a fire-engine red automobile so heavy with hardware it must have eaten eighteen dollars' worth of gasoline just coming.

That was twenty years ago, and folks mark it as the last dance ever thrown on the square in Johnson City. Red just couldn't get up the energy to try it again.

CHAPTER 16

Flab versus Ralph

I dress the way I do because of guys like Flab Blount and Uncle Glen, not Ralph Lauren.

And it hacks me for people to think otherwise.

The other morning Nanette and I were saying our goodbyes to the hill country, getting ready to turn the old Buick back toward Dallas and wind up our tour of Texas honky-tonks. We were having hamburgers for breakfast in this truck stop at Johnson City when I overheard a guy in the next booth make what I took to be a disparaging remark about my attire. He said to his friends, "Look at that New York cowboy."

I admit what I had on was a little heavy for summer — a black, 7X Beaver Resistol with a Las Vegas crush, black corduroy jeans and black Mexican riding heels — but I was in a Black Billy, mow 'em down mean hombre mood. The reason isn't important now. I will say it had to do with the glass windows of the Buick, which apparently for no good reason except age and brittleness — accented by the heat — suddenly dematerialized into a thousand cracks, leaving us with the prospect of trying to see through spider web-like panes on the long drive home. Nanette was sweet about it and tried to humor me, but the smart aleck in the next booth only made it worse. In such a mindset, I couldn't resist challenging the man. After, of course, checking his size and physical condition.

"What did you mean by that remark?" I asked, leveling him with my Lash LaRue look.

"Oh, nothing but the highest compliment to you, sir," he said nimbly. "It's the first Ralph Lauren look we've seen down here."

It was all his friends could do not to snicker in my face.

I wanted to draw my trusty Colt and blow him away, but instead I whimpered an apology to the waitress for not having enough money to tip her and limped away to confront the Buick, which waited outside like the Ayatollah Khomeini. On the way I told the guy off. I gave it to him straight. I may not be the genuine article, I let him know. But I was the genuine simulated article, which is a lot closer to the real thing than Ralph Lauren and all those radical chic phonies from the East Coast can claim. Besides, my real name wasn't Lipschitz. My real name was Billy Mack. Nuff said. I told the guy this in my mind. I didn't just out and out say it.

There was a time when I thought as a consolation I might become one of the beautiful people like Ralph Lauren, not because I really wanted to but because my public might demand it of me. It would be the price I had to pay for writing books that would not stay off the *New York Times* best-seller list. I would be back and forth between Dallas and New York, putting up with hangers-on like the Kennedy children and the Hemingway grandchildren, sparring with meatheads like Norman Mailer, having to go to Bloomingdale's when really all I wanted was a longneck at the Lone Star Cafe.

Thank God I had the sense to tone down my books and keep them within a limited circulation. I would have made a botch at being rich and chic. I've never known how to say it either. Is it chic as in bic, or chic as in chick, or chic as in sheik. No, not shake. I mean the old way of saying sheik. Sheek! Never mind. The point is I've never been able to read the beautiful people. I'm never quite sure what is in and what is out.

When Richard Avedon was in Dallas for his show at the museum, I didn't run down to Neiman-Marcus and deck myself out in Ralphie Baby's western collection before making my entrance. I was always taught that denim and leather and weather were fine for the corral and carousing, but that you put on a starched white shirt and tie and suit when you had some place real nice to go. Shoot. There's nothing spiffier than a fancy museum fling, so I did myself up proud, just the way Mother would have wanted, bless her memory.

I put on my shiny Sunday suit from Curlee's of Seguin, smacked down my cowlick with pomade, and went to Fair Park, where I felt like a perfect idiot. Fred Astaire couldn't have been more out of place in a John Wayne oat burner. Here I was dressed to the nines in my $65 suit with wide lapels, and there, all about me, were the beautiful people, and what were they wearing but boots and jeans and bandannas!

The fact that they were all going off to Buffalo Gap for a weekend of barbecue and beer made it more appropriate, but the irony would not go away. It was not too many years ago that I was asked to leave a party in Manhattan because I looked like I "had just been dragged in off the range." Little did they know that I hadn't been within light years of a cow, much less a herd of them. I dressed that way because that's what you wore when you were raised in places like Henderson, Graham, Rexroat, Seminole and White Deer. Our model was Uncle Glen.

Uncle Glen always said no matter how poor a man was, he ought to own the best in his woman, his hat and boots and bed. Because, he added with a rakish flourish, that's where a man spends most of his time.

That was true of Glen. He was a day late and a dollar short when it came to work, and no man spent more time stomping in honky-tonks and sneaking off to motels. He was a drunk and a ne'er-do-well, and when he died on the road of life trying to thumb a ride, we buried him with a sob of relief. But he left us one positive impression.

Glen was the handsomest road dog around, never the worse for the wear and tear of life on the drift. He wore handmade boots that were always polished, heavy cord khaki or gabardine pants and shirt, a belt to match his boots, and a 7X Beaver Stetson. I've forgotten the hair tonic and aftershave he wore, but he smelled so good and masculine that Mother said he ought to be outlawed and kept off the streets. His women? They were never up to snuff as far as we were concerned. And it looked like they owned him instead of him owning them. It goes without saying that his bed was usually a flea bag.

But Glen himself, the physical dude, was splendid, the first male in the family to show any concern about his dress. He brought to our five-and-dime lives a sense of style. It wasn't fashion. Glen wasn't up on anything much except the new Hank Williams song. Early on he donned a classically simple outfit that was right for him, and he stayed with it regardless of his circumstance. We buried him in it, his hat on his manly chest, and hoped that he would be a little less vulnerable to the ladies below, because that was certainly where he was going.

It is amazing how well you can see through spider web glass once you get used to it. Nanette and I made it clear across Texas and were on the final leg home when we decided to stop in Hillsboro and buy a couple of summer straws from Flab Blount. Flab used to sell hats and accessories to Uncle Glen. He's the 300-pound giant who runs the Brand-N-Iron Western Wear out on the interstate. He's also the town mayor, or was. Anyway, after Avedon, I was glad to see that Flab's prices were still twice as cheap as Ralph Lauren was getting at Bloomingdale's and Neiman's and Cutter Bill's.

"That figures," Flab said. "His is high-style stuff. You pay for the label and the flair, not the workaday lines that hold up to real wear and tear. You might disco in Ralphie Baby's clothes, but you wouldn't want to bulldog a steer."

Did Flab have anything in his store the beautiful people might be interested in?

"Yep," he said, "authenticity. Send 'em out here and I'll put a little manure on their boots."

Down in Woodsboro High, Elsie Fay French taught me never to end a sentence with a preposition, but I think Flab struck the right note for me to end this thing on. The only thing I would add is that after you step in a little cow doo, go honky-tonking. It's fun kicking that stuff around to the Cotton-Eyed Joe. Now, try the Oklahoma two-step. A one, a two, a three; a one, a two, a three; a one, a two. Slide, touch, kick. Attaway!

BOOK THREE

The Dances

*These dance steps and instructions are intended as a beginning guide.
Lessons are recommended to perfect the steps.
Many honky-tonks offer free lessons on certain nights.*

Waltz

The waltz sounds like the most unlikely dance to be found in a honky-tonk, but actually it's second only to the two-step in popularity.

It's an easy dance, once you get in the swing of it. Man and woman face each other, like in other slow dances, and clasp hands out from their bodies. (The man's left hand, the woman's right.) The woman puts her other arm around her man's shoulder (or she hooks her finger in his belt-loop) and the man holds his woman around the waist or cups his hand behind her neck. The man steps forward with his left foot (she back with her right) and then brings his right foot up next to it and puts his weight on that foot. He lifts his left foot slightly off the floor in a little step, and then sets it down again, lifting the right foot. So it's big step, little step, little step. One two three. Then start on your right foot. (The woman follows the man's steps, except reverse feet and backwards. It's fun to do the waltz in circles — you can show off that way — but the up-and-down motion of formal waltzing is left out of the country version. Think *glide*.

WALTZ
3 Beats with Each Lead Foot

Man's Part
Woman's Part is Reverse

Polka

There are more polkas than there are schottisches, but polka in a honky-tonk usually means one thing: round and round and round.

Partners face each other and take the same positions as for the two-step. Actually, the polka is similar to the two-step. It's the same dance, it just leaves one of the side steps out.

The man steps forward with his left foot (woman back on her right). He steps again on his right foot, she back on her left. He steps again on his left foot and brings his right next to it in a side step. (With the woman, as usual, it's reverse and backwards.) Then you repeat the steps. So its step, step, step, touch. Repeat. The only catch is the turning. That's what makes it the polka — the rotating of the couple while they are circling the dancefloor. It's kind of like the earth rotating on its axis while circling the sun. The thing that messes people up is they either get dizzy or the man gets so stuck in his forward motion he can't go backwards. (This goes reverse for women.) Polkas are fast, and the way to keep from getting dizzy is to keep your eyes fixed on some stationary object, turning your head to watch it until you can't anymore, then snapping your head around quick to get a glimpse of it over your other shoulder, staying glued till you can't anymore and, snap again. You've seen ballerinas do it. On second thought, maybe you haven't. As far as the changing directions goes, that's a matter of coordination and practice. Just keep twirling.

POLKA

4 Beats Each Lead Foot
Man's Part
Woman's Part is Reverse

COTTON-EYED JOE
Part B

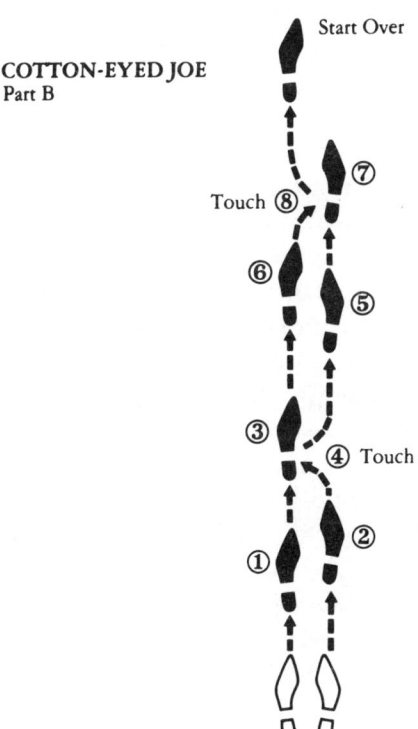

The Cotton-Eyed Joe

The Cotton-Eyed Joe is done, usually, to a particular song of the same name. You'll know the song when you hear the crowd screaming "Bullshit" at different intervals. Sometimes the Cotton-Eyed Joe dance is referred to as "The Bullshit."

Dancers for this one are side by side, with their arms around each other's waists. Woman is usually on her partner's right. (Lots of folks in dancehalls form long "chorus lines" for the Cotton-Eyed Joe, linking couples together at the shoulders.)

At the first part of the music, you'll make two small kicks with your left foot. Usually the first of these kicks crosses over the right ankle and the second is more straight out. Different people don't cross over at all, some do on both kicks. Make your own style. After the two kicks, you'll step backward on your left foot. Then take two more steps back, and left. These are quick steps back, so you may not travel far. In fact the second step may result in placing your right foot next to your left, which took the first step backward. Years back, people used to merely stomp three times instead of moving backward, but reverse seems to be the new trend.

Next, repeat that series three more times, making it four in total. Kick, kick, step, step, step. After the fourth time you'll take a step forward with your left foot and begin a series of eight Polka steps. (Four with the left foot leading, four with the right foot leading — alternating feet. See Polka Steps.) Do this, alternating feet, for a total of eight steps. The faster you go — and the tempo of the Cotton-Eyed Joe accelerates throughout the song — this particular step will become more of a sliding skip.

After you finish the eight forward steps, start back with the first kicking sequence. Kick, kick, step, step, step, four times and then start the eight Polka steps again. Repeat both sequences until the song ends or you run out of steam, whichever comes first. (This sucker gets *fast!*)

In some honky tonks you'll see people doing incredibly fancy versions of the Cotton-Eyed Joe. The man will generally do the regular steps, but his female partner will be spinning and weaving and doing all sorts of stunts. Pay no attention. They're just show-offs.

COTTON-EYED JOE
Specialty Dance

Part A

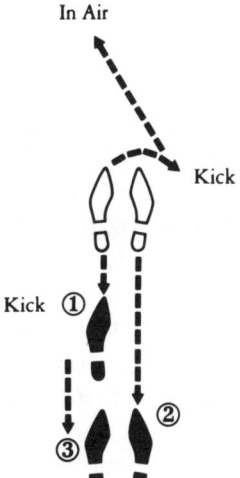

Repeat 3 Times
Alternating Feet

Part B   See Polka

Sweetheart Schottische

There are umpteen different schottisches in dance manuals. The Danish Schottische, the Ping Pong (?) Schottische, the Military Schottische, the Old Southern Schottische, the Sweetheart Schottische, the Rosemary Schottische. That doesn't help you when someone approaches in a dancehall and asks, "Can you schottische?" Don't ask, "Which one?" There is only one in the honky-tonks of today, and it goes like this:

The dance is done with the man and the woman side by side, with arms around each other's waists. Step left with the left foot. Cross behind it with the right foot. Step left again with left foot, and skip (subtly, please. These places are crowded.) with the right foot. There is a little spring on the left foot when the right is skipping. (Skipping foot, right in this case, is on the ground.)

Repeat the sequence to the right. Step right with right foot, then left crosses behind, then right with right foot again and the left skips. (This all goes at a slight diagonal.) Then skip forward four times, stepping first on left foot, then right then left and then right again. These are small skips again, and the knee of the leg that's up in the air should be brought straight up so your thigh is parallel to the floor. Then repeat sequence. It's crisscross to the left, skip; crisscross to the right, skip. Skip, skip, skip, skip.

You may feel like an idiot doing this one, it gets faster, just like the Cotton-Eyed Joe does — but at least it's not the Bunny Hop.

SWEETHEART SCHOTTISCHE
Specialty Dance

Steps Represent Foot on the Ground, Other Foot is Up in the Air as in a Skip.

Part A

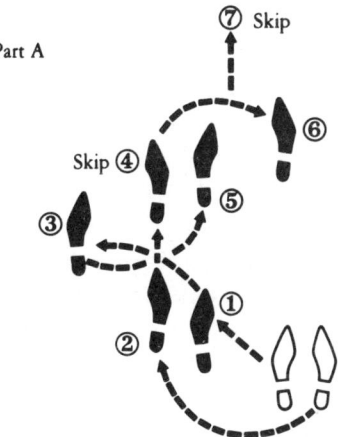

Part B

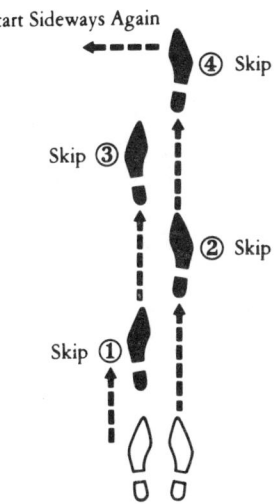

Two-Step

The two-step is probably the most popular of the old country dances, and the one you'll most often see in modern honky-tonks. As in most all the dances, dancers will dance counterclockwise in a circle, sometimes around a post or ornament placed in the center of the dancefloor.

Dancers should face each other for the-two step, like for a slow dance. The real expert two-steppers will take a stylized pose — the man will cup his hand behind the woman's neck (instead of behind her back) and the woman will hook a finger in her partner's belt-loop instead of putting her arm around him. Then they clasp hands with their free arms. This gives a special look to the two-step when it's done fast. Dancers keep their bodies particularly rigid during the fast version, moving only their feet.

To do the two-step, the male partner begins by stepping forward with his left foot, then his right foot, then his left again. These are three straight, normal walking steps that move him forward. His partner should step back with her right foot, then left, then right. At the end of the last step the man should bring the toe of his right boot to rest lightly next to his left foot. Some people don't do it with a touch, but use a sliding motion to get the right foot next to the left. A lot depends on the speed at which the dance is being done.

After touching the right foot to the left, the right foot should return to its position, and the left foot will slide over, or touch over, next to it. For the woman it is opposite feet, matching her partner. Then repeat the three steps.

Actually, it's easiest to think of this dance in sets of two steps, since that's what it's called. First you step forward normally twice, left and right. Then you step left, touch (or slide with right foot to touch) then step right, touch with left. There is a slight side-to-side motion on the glide steps and the normal steps will be forward motion, but gliding, feet always skimming the floor.

TWO STEP
6 Counts Done to 4 beat Music

Man's Part
Woman's Part is Reverse

⑦ Repeat #1

Slide